A Pocketful
of Hope

To our unborn baby girl.
May you inhabit a world of hope …

A Pocketful of Hope

An A–Z of answers
to life's big questions

**Pat Allerton
The Portable Priest**

First published in Great Britain in 2022 by Yellow Kite Books
An Hachette UK company

1

Copyright © Patrick Allerton 2022

The right of Patrick Allerton to be identified as the Author
of the Work has been asserted by him in accordance with the
Copyright, Designs and Patents Act 1988.

Unless otherwise stated, all Bible references are taken from
the New International Version (NIV)

Illustrations © Charlotte Trounce 2022

A CIP catalogue record for this title is available from the British Library

Hardback ISBN 978 1 529 39528 0
eBook ISBN 978 1 529 39529 7

Typeset in Adobe Caslon Pro by Goldust Design

Printed and bound in Great Britain by Clays Ltd, Elcograf S.p.A.

Hodder & Stoughton policy is to use papers that are natural, renewable
and recyclable products and made from wood grown in sustainable for-ests.
The logging and manufacturing processes are expected to conform to the
environmental regulations of the country of origin.

Yellow Kite
Hodder & Stoughton Ltd
Carmelite House
50 Victoria Embankment
London EC4Y 0DZ

www.yellowkitebooks.co.uk

Contents

All of us need hope.
It's just knowing where to find it ...

This isn't a book for religious people. (But by all means read it if you are!)

This isn't even a book for those with faith, although I hope it encourages you if you have it.

This is a book for the seeking ones. The searchers. Those who know there must be more ...

Introduction

I was recently at a lunch where it came up in conversation that I was writing a book. A chap I'd just met then naturally asked me, 'Fiction or non-fiction?' With a wry smile, I replied, 'While many might call it the former, I believe it belongs in the latter category!'

We live in an age where more and more people are saying something like, 'I'm not religious, but I am spiritual.' This book is for those people and it will look to engage with that space. It seeks to make the invisible, visible; the spiritual, physical – putting flesh on the bones of that idea.

In all that follows, I simply want people to feel like they are getting a better idea of who God is and the difference following Jesus can make in their lives. At the very least, he was as wise a man who's ever walked the earth, so he's not a bad mentor or guru to have. At the most, he's God incarnate and has the power to change our lives. But people will have the freedom to take or leave whatever they choose from this book. My role is merely to be a middleman, helping people encounter the words and spirit of the person who's not only changed my life, but millions of others for 2,000 years.

'Hope' isn't just a nice thought or a warm fuzzy feeling.

It's not a 'strategy', as someone once said. Where true, hope is genuinely life-changing and nothing can compare with it.

So I invite you to come on a journey of heart and soul. Open yourself to what might be. Ask God to draw near to you. And come: dip your toe into the water …

My Story

I didn't grow up in a Christian home. In fact, there wasn't talk of religion at all. It's not that I was opposed to God or belief in him; I guess it's simply that, up until the age of 18, he simply wasn't on my radar; the whole thing just seemed irrelevant. But then something began to change. I started to have questions I just couldn't answer. Questions like, 'Where do we come from?', 'What's the point?', 'What happens when we die?', 'If there's a God, what does he think of me and, more importantly, am I in trouble?' (I was pretty sure I must be.)

My best friend Dave was a Christian, having come to faith in Jesus two years earlier, and I remember grilling him with all these questions. Poor guy. But, then again, now I know how excited he must have been that something was clearly stirring in me. He took me to church in London a couple of times and to Christian Union at school. I remember finding the music and singing, although beautiful and uplifting, strange, because I had no idea what they were singing about or whom they were singing it to. To me, it just seemed like a massive version of corporate karaoke, singing words that were on a big screen.

But when the preaching started, it all began to make sense. It was like they were speaking just to me and somehow knew the questions I had. And so my curiosity grew. Then in the Easter holidays of our last year at school, Dave invited me on a Christian holiday camp. I didn't have a lot going on (other than revision, and who wants that?), so after some consideration I said I'd go. And it was there that everything changed.

I arrived at the camp and immediately sensed something different about the people there and their interactions with one another. It was like these teenagers had a light and a joy in them that, deep down, I knew I just didn't have. Maybe you've got a Christian friend and you know exactly what I'm talking about. It made me hungry to find out why. There were sessions with singing and teaching, which were fine, but on the third day I heard a message that really rocked my world. A young man in his twenties gave a simple explanation about the evidence for the resurrection. Now, I wasn't completely new to Christianity: I'd always sung in school choirs, so had been in chapel most days of the week from the age of 7 until about 14, when I decided I was just too cool to be a chorister and couldn't be seen wearing a cassock and surplice by my mates, so I quit. But still, I must have spent close to 1,000 hours in church services by then – enough to know it was all about Jesus. But I'd never heard an explanation like this before.

Simply put, we were presented with evidence for the historical and bodily resurrection of Jesus Christ. The young man showed, using clear logic, that Jesus had *really* died and that he'd really been buried, and that, as is central to the Christian faith, he had really risen again three days later. In other words, he hadn't 'revived' in the cool of the tomb and run away, as some sceptics suggest. His (terrified) disciples hadn't nicked the body; the authorities hadn't nicked the body; robbers hadn't nicked the body (if so, they left the only thing that was valuable

– his grave clothes with all the expensive spices in them – and, besides which, the tomb was guarded by crack Roman soldiers). Add to that Jesus' recorded appearances to his disciples over the next 40 days – on one occasion to 500 people at the same time (hard to believe that that many people hallucinated together) – the transformation of cowering disciples into fearless preachers who'd die for their faith, his fulfilment of over 300 prophecies written before his birth and the continued existence of the Church some 2,000 years later, with millions claiming to experience the reality and presence of Jesus today, I found this young man's argument for the resurrection and divinity of Jesus Christ compelling.

More than that, I found it filled with hope. One of the things that drove me on in my quest to find deeper meaning – I looked into other faiths and philosophies too – was my struggle to accept that we are all just here by accident; that this breathtaking, awesome, mysterious universe came about by pure chance. Yes, I accept whatever science can prove. But behind the 'how' questions, there are always the 'why' questions, and these were the more pressing ones for me. Perhaps they are for you, too. And in this simple presentation of the evidence for the resurrection, I felt the ground beneath me shaking and the heavens above me opening. (Not literally, I'm trying to be poetic.) I was buzzing with excitement. Because in that moment I knew that, if this was true, if Jesus had truly risen, if he was physically alive today, albeit in heaven where we can't now see him, then it meant that I could know him, that all my questions could be answered. It meant that God was real, and that I might be able to connect with him. I don't know why I'd not felt like doing this for the first 18 years of my life – maybe I was too distracted. All I knew was that, in that moment,

I was filled with an inexplicable hope. Or at least, the hope of hope.

I went back to my room that night and proceeded to read the Bible in bed for a bit; something I'd never done before. After a few minutes, I knew the moment had come – it was time to take a step of faith. So, I started to pray. It felt so foolish, like I was talking to the ceiling, but I did it anyway. And, in essence, what I said was this, 'God, I don't know you yet. But I want to. I believe that you're real. Please come into my life. I turn away from the stuff I know is wrong. You can take the (hoped-for) sex, and drugs, and "rock and roll", everything I look to for security and identity. I just want you. Please, come into my life.'

I've always said that, in that moment, I felt as exposed and vulnerable as I ever have done. Because I knew that if nothing happened, if I didn't experience anything, then I may as well have given up my search for God, because I didn't know how to offer him more. I didn't know how to be any more 'open'. It felt like a spiritual version of that trust exercise that teams do, where they get you to stand up and hold your arms out to the sides, and then fall backwards, trusting that your friend or colleague will catch you. Do you know the one? I saw a YouTube video of some guy doing it once, but instead of falling backwards he fell forwards – not good. But, either way, it's a scary step and a leap of faith, but there's no other way and you have to commit.

Once I'd prayed, and I'll never forget this, it was as if a surge of electricity filled my body, like liquid love was poured into my heart. It was around midnight and I was lying in my bed, and the physical sensation was such that I was arching up on my heels and shoulder blades, experiencing this ecstatic spiritual moment. It's hard to describe, but as that happened, I just knew that everything I was looking for – every question, worry or fear, every hope or dream or desire, everything – was answered, found and satisfied. I knew then that God was real. I'd found him, or he'd found me, and things would never be the same.

How I became
'The Portable Priest'
~

That was 25 years ago, and although life hasn't been a bed of roses since, although I've had my ups and downs and questions (who hasn't?), I can honestly say that I wouldn't change it for anything. Jesus changes everything. He really is alive. You really can know him. I understand how weird it is to hear that because I say that as someone who, for many years, didn't believe and as someone whose family doesn't (yet!) share his faith. But hey, I don't think you'd be reading this book if you weren't at least open to the idea of there being more ... and why wouldn't there be? After all, I mean, goodness, there are so many wonders and mysteries in the universe, it's not ridiculous to imagine that there's something or someone behind it all – a designer or creator. Quite the opposite, I'd suggest. And, if there is, well, why would they leave themselves without witness? Without some record or word about themselves? Surely they'd want their creation to know them? Why else would they have made us?

This is the journey I went on and that's exactly what I discovered. I learnt that the whole Christian thing is simply about relationship and connecting with the one who made us. In a nutshell, God loves us and created us to know him and enjoy his love. That's why he sent Jesus, his Son, in human flesh, to reveal what God is like. And, goodness, he's beautiful. A God who'd lay down his life for us; yes, for you and me, despite what we've done? Are you joking? How loving is such a God? How humble is such a creator?

And, you see, long story short, it's really that message that took me to the streets during the first Covid-19 lockdown. When churches were closed and we were all sheltering at home – many of us separated from loved ones, anxious about the future, perhaps sick or grieving a loss – I took to the streets of London, playing a hymn and leading a prayer. I went out around 64 times in all, starting on the Portobello Road in my parish (geographical patch) of Notting Hill, west London, but then going on to visit many other streets. I also set up shop outside hospitals and care homes, even a prison on one occasion. I'd go around on my hired 3-wheel cargo bike (generously sponsored by some friends) as part of my one hour of daily exercise, plugging my (very loud) 1-KW sound system into a petrol generator (so as to maintain social distancing), and then I'd kick off.

I'd start each time by saying, 'Good morning/afternoon, people of … my name is Pat and I'm a vicar in the Church of England. I wonder if you could give me just five minutes or so of your time [it was usually eight, but I hoped no one was counting]. These are challenging and difficult days that we're facing and I've just felt led to head out onto the streets to try to bring a bit of hope, to lift our spirits, to bring us together for just a moment. My thinking is that if people can't go to church, maybe church should go to the people. So if you'd like to come to your windows, or doorways, I'd love to invite you to enjoy a favourite hymn, which many of you may know – please feel free to sing along. After that, we'll hold a moment of silence, where we can bring to mind people we know who are struggling right now; people we know who are suffering; anyone sick with Covid at this time; anyone grieving the loss of a loved one; anyone who works in the NHS or is a key worker; anyone weighed down by worry or anxiety. After that, and only if you'd like to, we can pray the Lord's Prayer together, committing them, and our world, to God.'

That would basically be my spiel each time, which I'd seek to convey with gentleness and respect. After all, I realised that what I was doing might not be loved by everyone, and that it was somewhat intrusive on their homes and ears! The key thing to know if you're using an amplified device that can be heard up to a kilometre in any direction is that you need to keep things short, and you need to be respectful. Especially when you, quite literally, have a captive audience.

As we pulled onto the Portobello Road in my car that very first time (this was before I hired my bike), I suddenly realised I hadn't picked a hymn, but I instinctively knew it should be 'Amazing Grace', just because it's loved equally by people of all faiths and none. It would have a resonance with people, whether they sang it last week or hadn't sung it since their childhood. And it carries a wonderful message of hope for those difficult times:

Amazing grace
How sweet the sound
That saved a wretch like me
I once was lost, but now am found
Was blind, but now I see.

My housemate, Chris, and I rapidly searched Spotify, looking for the right vibe. We listened to a few and thought, *no/almost /mmm* … before my eyes alighted on 'Judy Collins'. I pressed 'play' in the car – goosebumps immediately. It was haunting and beautiful, a stunning rendition of that old, favourite hymn. I hadn't heard of Judy before, but my mum later informed me that she was a folk singer from the seventies. I loved that.

That first day, we parked up on a very quiet street and set up our kit. We had a small battery pack to power the speakers, but, no sooner had I announced our arrival and begun to introduce myself, the battery pack gave up the ghost! The speakers were just too powerful. So, it was back to the church to find more kit. We realised that we'd need mains power, so grabbed an extension lead and went back to our spot, this time knocking on a congregation member's door and safely handing over the end of the lead for them to plug in. Finally, we were up and running! All I can say is, that was a make-or-break moment for me. As the hymn played, echoing around the streets of Notting Hill, we began to see dozens of faces appearing at windows and doorways, people looking on with a mix of curiosity and enjoyment (and possibly other feelings too). But, let's be honest, there wasn't a lot else going on in those early lockdown months, so any distraction was welcome. But as the hymn came in to land, I didn't know what to expect. Would it be indifference? Would it be anger and rejection? Would it be a smile but nothing more?

As the last note melted into the sunset evening air, I was happy, and relieved, to hear a ripple of applause. Better than rotten tomatoes, I thought. But then that ripple built and got louder, with even some whoops and cheering too. The people seemed to have enjoyed it! We held some silence before I then encouraged those who'd like to to pray the Lord's Prayer, that tells us of a God in heaven who's not aloof or indifferent, who's not distant or uncaring, but is our Father, and who showed his love by sending us his Son, Jesus Christ. I quoted Psalm 23, saying how, at this time, it felt like the whole world was walking through the 'valley of the shadow of death', but how there's a Good Shepherd who wants to walk that path with us, one who'll never leave us nor forsake us, one who came to give us life. And then we prayed. At the end, I thanked them for having me, and for tolerating a very loud speaker system. There were claps and cheers again, with cries of 'encore' and 'come back soon' to boot, which I duly did a couple more times. I hope they didn't regret it!

But the key thing was that the format seemed to work. I felt alive doing it and people seemed to be remarkably open to it happening. But, more importantly, I believe it brought some hope. And so a brand-new ministry was born! Where before, my Instagram name was @theportobellopriest, deliberately chosen to enable me to communicate with my parish and allow them to eavesdrop on church business, some clever journalist rechristened me @theportablepriest, and the name stuck! And, to be honest, I'm glad it did, as it actually captured much more effectively the nature of what I was up to.

Moving beyond my parish, I headed all over London during those next 10 weeks, going wherever I felt led or was invited. One street wanted me to visit so they could support a neighbour who'd lost her husband to Covid but couldn't have a proper funeral. Another couple invited me to come to the care home opposite their flat. One friend quickly suggested that I should go to hospitals, as that's where this service and message was needed most. How right she was! It was always the greatest honour to share my thoughts outside a hospital, although I always wondered how much sound could actually get into those giant, sealed buildings, which is why it was such a blessing to receive occasional feedback over Instagram or some other way. Having brought a hymn and a prayer to Charing Cross Hospital, I was deeply moved to receive a couple of messages shortly afterwards, one from a nurse who said, 'I was doing a shift yesterday in Charing Cross and heard this and I was balling [sic] crying. At the time I was in a side room with a patient who was sadly coming to the end of her life due to her not being able to fight the battle with Covid-19. I cannot thank you enough for the peace that this song brought me and that patient at that difficult time.'

Someone else messaged me saying, 'I am not a religious person, but I wanted to thank you for what you did on Thursday night outside Charing Cross Hospital. My uncle was in there at the time and passed away, alone, the following morning, due to coronavirus. Knowing he could've heard this on his last night on this planet brings tears to my eyes and warmth to my heart. Thank you, from the bottom of my heart.'

Messages like these made it all worthwhile. And I'd do it all again. Because people need hope. People need comfort. And God wants to meet with them. Is there more I wish I could have said or done? Yes. Did I always get it right? No. I was sworn at, shouted at, turned off on two occasions, once by a lady who simply asked, 'Have you any idea how disruptive you're being?' Well, there was only one honest answer to that. She then proceeded to pull the plug from my extension lead, plunging us into silence! Her daughter then got in touch over Instagram to apologise, which was very kind of her. But despite all that, I am still so pleased that I stepped out in faith and did what I felt called to do, because it brought some hope at a difficult time, and there's nothing more precious than that.

And that's sort of what I feel, too, with this book.

Rooted in faith and spirituality, this book seeks to offer uplifting thoughts and meditations on a wide range of topics and challenges we all face. Without being preachy or pushy, I hope to bring you into contact with the perspective of faith and the difference it can make in our lives.

In Jesus' own time, some believed, others didn't, but countless people came into contact with him. They walked with him, spoke with him, discussed their lives with him, watched and listened to him. However they then decided to respond to him – whether they believed and followed, or didn't and just walked on – was completely up to them. But one thing is certain: everyone was touched, everyone was challenged, everyone was intrigued – and many were changed.

So, wherever you are on the mountain range of faith – whether close to the summit or down in the valley, or whether you don't even believe that mountains exist (!) – my hope and prayer is that this book somehow touches and speaks to you.

Alpha

Well, it had to begin this way didn't it? The beginning of the alphabet. The first step on the journey. When you're writing an A to Z of something (or 'Alpha' to 'Omega' in the Greek), this is the natural place to start.

But the honest truth is that, with regard to this book and my very real sense of impostor syndrome writing it, 'A' should perhaps be pronounced 'Eh?' Because the reality is, I'm just not sure I feel up to the task, or equipped or qualified to do it! In so many ways, my life is a mess and my inner world a strange mix of shadow and light, of holy and profane, that I feel I've nothing to give. So at the thought of writing this book, so much within me cries out, 'Eh?!'

But then, perhaps that's precisely the point. Because isn't that exactly how many of us feel when beginning a new venture or initiative? We often don't feel up to it, question if we've got it, worry about failure or how others will perceive us. But if we listen to the 'eh?' instead of just starting out at 'A', then we'd never accomplish anything. Imagine if, in 1953, mountaineers Tenzing Norgay and Sir Edmund Hillary had listened to the naysayers or that inner voice of doubt; perhaps we'd never have known for sure if Everest could indeed be conquered.

Imagine if Neil Armstrong and the genius minds at NASA had felt the moon was a bridge too far, if they'd all have gone home early for tea instead of pushing the bounds of what's humanly possible. Or if Mozart hadn't picked up that violin (or was it a piano?), or Serena Williams that tennis racquet …

Or just imagine if *you* hadn't done … or gone … or said … or written …

But it all begins with 'A'. It all begins at the beginning. So crack on, make a start, get going, and know that there's purpose and meaning in everything. Because, ultimately, it's all held by the Alpha and the Omega, the beginning and the end, the one who lives forever: Jesus Christ.

He's where my courage comes from. He's where I find my hope. And I'll be speaking about him a bit as we go, because, without him, well, quite frankly, I've got nothing to say or give. So forgive me if I do, but I think he could help you too …

Anxiety

Goodness life can be overwhelming! I mean, the world's just so big and so loud and so demanding. So many voices, so many decisions, so much opportunity. So many choices of coats, or shoes (or handbags I imagine!), let alone jobs or places to live or whom to spend your life with. And to think we only get one chance: YOLO! It's enough to stress out even the most horizontal of personalities ...

I follow a very amusing account on Instagram called 'VeryBritishProblems'. I recommend you give it a go! In it, they look at familiar British expressions and idioms and then translate what they really mean. A recent example shared how 'Yeah, could do' actually means, 'No'. So true! Well, I came across one that says the following:

'I'm off to bed.'
Translation: 'I'm off to lie down and worry about the
future and also to worry about every mistake I've ever made,
no matter how great or small, and to go over all the embar-
rassing moments from my past that I'll never ever forget.
Night night.'

This may be a joke, but it taps into exactly what we're seeing: an exponential increase in anxiety and mental health issues. It's almost as if, the more advanced and capable our society and world becomes, the more we struggle to know how to handle it. Perhaps you've known it in your own life. When your breathing gets shallow, your eyes start to sting, you feel isolated and alone, and a new day heralds fresh dread.

So how do we find peace? How do we still our hearts and the rampant anxiety that would seek to consume us? How do we find balance and equilibrium?

When I was a kid and felt car sick in the back seat once, I remember my aunt saying to me, 'fix your eyes on the horizon, it's the one thing that doesn't change'. Life can feel a bit like that, like we're in the back of a car travelling winding roads, not knowing where we're going, or if there's even anyone driving!

When we feel tossed by the storms and waves of life, we need to plant our feet on rock. We need an anchor for our souls. All I can say is, for me, Jesus is that rock, that anchor, that horizon. He brings me peace, he calms my nerves, he restores my soul. And he promises to do that for anyone who comes to him …

Some of my favourite words of his are, 'Come to me, all you who are weary and burdened, and I will give you rest. Take my yoke upon you and learn from me, for I am gentle and humble in heart, and you will find rest for your souls. For my yoke is easy and my burden is light' (Matthew 11:28–30).

I love them because it's so opposite to what we might expect when we think of God. So often, people think that he'll make things worse, make us feel bad and, if anything, load us up with burdens. We certainly don't expect him to take them off! But that's exactly what happens. Somehow, when I pray, I experience his presence and what seemed heavy before doesn't seem so heavy anymore. I mean, those things are still there, but it's like God is helping me carry them.

Imagine two oxen (or other animals) harnessed together side by side by a piece of wood, called a yoke, in order to pull something heavy. The two animals share their burden, each pulling their share of the weight. But when it comes to faith, it's different. Jesus invites us to take his yoke upon ourselves, but he says that it's easy and that his burden is light. How can this be? Well, it's because he does the heavy lifting! Although we're yoked to him, he's always one step, one foot, one inch ahead of us, which means the weight and burden falls on him, and we're just there for the ride. It's not that the issues or challenges that we face aren't still there, it's just that we can know his presence with us in them, and a peace 'which transcends all understanding' (Philippians 4:7). Not that it's always easy, mind you! He'll take you places that might be hard and stretch your heart until it feels it might break. But as hard as it is, it's good and it feels right. Like it's what you were always made to do and be.

What I'm saying is, bring your burdens and anxieties to God. He wants to give you rest. Isn't that what your heart longs for deep down? And isn't that the last thing this world seems to give? I sometimes feel like it's just impossible to find true rest – that life's just too full, and fast, and hectic. My brain feels like a phone with no more memory! I have to delete 'apps' to make more space.

The yoke of this world can seem cruel and heavy – it often lacks grace, forgiveness or kindness. Just look at Twitter for goodness sake! People are scared to express an opinion. It's very unrelaxing … And it certainly doesn't feel liberating.

But through faith we find a different path. God sees the

things we carry. The regrets and pain from our past. The fear of what's to come. He sees those worries that niggle, the anxiety that won't leave us alone. We fret about the future, because we don't know what it holds. And then that eats into the present, stealing joy and hope and peace. Faith doesn't exempt us from suffering or heavy burdens, but it does mean we've got God to help us carry them. He'd love to take them off our shoulders or at least let us know he's there. And when you invite him into your life, there's a glorious exchange that happens: we bring him our weariness, he gives us his strength; we bring him our burdens, he gives us rest for our souls. Doesn't that sound good?

There's a beautiful verse in the Bible that says, 'You have not given me into the hands of the enemy but have set my feet in a spacious place' (Psalm 31:8). I don't know about you, but I want that spacious place. I *need* that spacious place! God knows how to take us there and how to deliver us from the enemy – anxiety.

We may not know what the future holds, but we can know who holds the future. God is the unmoving rock. The unchanging horizon. The anchor for our souls. And you can come to him right now.

Authenticity

It's funny to note how TV programmes have changed since reality TV shows like *Big Brother* and *Love Island* shifted trends and expectations. It's as if we suddenly realised that we enjoy watching something that's rooted in reality – in real problems and emotions – just as much as we do something that's acted; indeed, possibly more so. I guess because we don't quite know which way it's going to go, but also because we increasingly value authenticity – people being their true and transparent selves – over hype or façade. And, deep down, we want that too. (OK, I know we might not *always* get that in those shows, but you know what I mean!)

We all long to live lives of genuine honesty and authenticity, but the pressure of social norms and fitting in, the 'should-ing' placed on us by society and culture, often squeezes us into its mould. And the thing about us humans is we're great mimics and imitators, so when we see what works or what's socially acceptable to others, we get right to work on impersonating it. We create masks and versions of ourselves, producing the requisite one for the setting we're in. But the problem with masks is that, when two of them meet, the connection isn't genuine or stable, as the 'real' people behind them haven't truly come into contact. It genuinely becomes possible to be two people at the same time.

As always, the Greeks had a word for it – 'hypokrites', which means 'an actor' or 'a stage player' (which gives us the English word, hypocrite). The original Greek word is a compound of two other words that mean 'an interpreter from underneath'. Strange, you might think, but not so when you understand that actors back then wore large masks, visible to the audience, to indicate what character they were playing, thus interpreting the story from underneath their masks.

Do you sometimes feel like that? Like you're playing a part and wearing a mask? I know I used to wear them – desperate to be liked, desperate to win and be seen as 'successful', convinced my identity and the world's acceptance of me somehow lay in that. I became a brilliant actor – not literally on the stage, but treading the boards of life, giving people what I thought they wanted, to secure what I thought I needed. 'Fake it till you make it' is a well-known expression these days, but have you really won if it's not really you?

We all long to be truly known and fully accepted for who we are. But when the world looks uncertain and we're not sure how we'll be received, it often feels safer to just stay behind the mask, to interpret life from 'underneath'. But such a path isn't life at all. There must be a better way.

For me, the most freeing truth in the world is to know that God knows everything about me and yet he loves me nonetheless! And I do mean *everything*. Let's be honest, he'd be a pretty rubbish God if he didn't – 'omniscience' is kinda crucial to the job description! The trouble is, people go round thinking that they can somehow hide their stuff from him or, rather, they're nervous to come to him because they're scared they'll be rejected 'if he really knew ...' Well, I've got news for you folks: he already does, and it still doesn't put him off. In fact, if anything, it *attracts* him to you. Because he's a rescuer, a fixer-upper, a redeemer and a saviour. He's not put off by your 'stuff' and there's no mess he can't deal with. He knows you to the depths of your soul, but he still loves you to the sky.

There's a beautiful psalm in the Bible that speaks of God's complete knowledge of us (Psalm 139:1–4). I encourage you to read the whole thing, but here's how it starts:

You have searched me, Lord,
and you know me.
You know when I sit and when I rise;
you perceive my thoughts from afar.
You discern my going out and my lying down;
you are familiar with all my ways.
Before a word is on my tongue
you, Lord, know it completely.

The psalm ends with the following words (Psalm 139:23–24):

Search me, God, and know my heart;
test me and know my anxious thoughts.
See if there is any offensive way in me,
and lead me in the way everlasting.

There is a better way to live than wearing a mask. It's the way of authenticity, and it opens up when you know you're loved ...

Blessing

'#blessed' is a favourite thing nowadays, but what does it mean and how can we be it?

When you stop to think about it, life really is a gift. I mean, did you know that the chances of *precisely* you being here at all are 1 in 10 to the power of 2,685,000. Err … say what buddy? I'm with you. But all we need to know is that's a pretty big number! In fact, it's a number with 2,685,000 zeros after it. That's enough zeros to fill a 1000-page book. In other words, it's about as likely as 2 million people getting together to play a game of trillion-sided dice (just go with it) and each rolling *exactly* the same number at *exactly* the same time!

To say it's a miracle you're here is a massive understatement.

And that's before we add in the chances of there being a universe at all, or a planet able to support intelligent, conscious life … And to think we can order pizza from our phones!

Talk about wonder. Talk about mystery. It's almost as if something or someone wanted us here. That's why, for me, it takes more faith to believe that there isn't a creator than that there is. The maths just doesn't add up otherwise.

I don't believe that we are here by chance. We are not just an accident. There is a deep, deep magic at work. There is design and purpose behind it all, which means we can dare to say 'thank you'. Thank you for the beauty. Thank you for the gifts. Thank you for the untold blessings that we enjoy every day. The sunshine breaking through, the snow-topped mountain peaks, the smile of a loved one, rain on a hot day, Wi-Fi that works, perfectly cooked steak, the cry of a newborn baby, art, literature, music, food, wine, birds and puppies. I mean, the list could go on and on …

Blessing – from the one who made it all – showering down on each of us. What a gift, if we'd just stop to recognise it.

And the mind-blowing truth of it all is that this same God who made the universe made you and me as well. Not just in a general sense, where he 'wound the clock up' and let it go, keeping an eye on things from a distance but not really fussed about specifics – which eighteenth-century philosophers called 'deism'. No, the Bible tells us that even the very hairs on our head are numbered, meaning that God knows us better than we know ourselves and is interested in every detail of our lives. (I know, for some, counting the hairs on our head isn't a very big job, but I think you get the picture.)

For me, knowing God is the greatest blessing of all. It's as if heaven and earth come into alignment and your destiny opens up. When you're connected to the blesser, then you're resourced to be a blessing. You hear words of life, you pass them on; you receive a touch of love, you love your neighbour; you're forgiven, you forgive. This is the true and spiritual circle of life. And the beautiful thing? We can all be involved – from the richest to the poorest, from the weakest to the strongest.

Mother Teresa was once interviewed by *Hello!* magazine (Issue 324, 1 October 1994). She was asked the question, 'Is it only the affluent who give?' She replied, 'No, even the poorest of the poor give. The other day a very poor beggar came up to me and said, "Everyone gives to you and I also want to give you twenty paisa" – which is about two pence. I thought to myself, what do I do? If I take it he won't have anything to eat, but if I don't take it I would hurt him so much. So I took it, and he was so happy because he had given to Mother Teresa of Calcutta to help the poor. Giving cleans the heart and helps you get closer to God. You get so much back in return.'

So many go through life with their heads down, blinkers on, seeing only mud and dust. Lift your eyes and look around you. See the sunrise and the stars. Let the light of God's grace restore your wonder as you connect with your creator. You're not here by chance. You have a purpose. You're made to be blessed and be a blessing.

Brokenness

All of us are broken, be it physically, emotionally, mentally or spiritually. It's probably not what we want to hear, we may do our best to cover it up, we might even deny it to ourselves, but the truth of the matter is, we are broken. Admitting to our brokenness feels hard and risky because we live in a world where 'strength' seems to win and get rewarded. Where those who've 'got it together' come out on top. Where broken, imperfect people all too often get rejected like second-hand toys.

And so we put up walls that say we're fine and that we're strong. *No leaks or cracks with this one, nothing to see here …*

The problem is it's just not true. If we continue to deny our brokenness then we begin to inhabit a lie. We begin to build our foundations on sand and, as the biblical parable goes, 'The rain came down, the streams rose, and the winds blew and beat against that house, and it fell with a great crash' (Matthew 7:27).

But what if we chose to embrace our brokenness?

The Japanese have a centuries-old practice called 'kintsugi' that is part of a broader philosophy of embracing the beauty of human flaws. In it, they take broken pots, the kind that many of us would probably throw out, and repair them by mixing lacquer with gold and bringing the cracks to life. They don't patch up or hide the broken parts; they make them the focus. The result? The pots end up even more beautiful than before.

This is the wonderful news: God accepts us with our broken bits; the parts we'd rather hide. He's not put off. He's not scared. He won't reject us. As long as we're willing to bring our whole selves to him, he can work with what we've got. Just look at what he did with five loaves and two fish (he fed 5,000 people, just in case you didn't know …).

So what are your broken bits today? The parts of you you'd rather hide? Because it's there he wants to meet us and it's there he can bind us up.

I love it (well I don't love it, but you'll see my point) when a small kid gets an 'owee' and runs to their parent to 'kiss it better'. You don't see kids 'suck it up' very often, keep a stiff upper lip or pretend like nothing happened. No! There's normally a short pause while an intake of breath is taken, before a shrill cry or scream to alert said parent, swiftly followed by hugs and kisses. At least, that's what good parenting should look like I guess! And it's exactly the same in the spiritual life. We get knocks and bruises, sometimes things break, but God is always there to embrace and hold us. All he needs is for us to come and be completely honest with him.

We should all recognise how beautiful brokenness can be. Do you have any scars? I have a scar on my cheek caused by an excited Labrador jumping up and catching its claw in my (very soft) cheek as I played 'British Bulldog' between two sofas at a friend's house aged five. My fault, not the dog's! But for years I hated this scar. I didn't like the way it curved. And yet now, I love it. A smile line now comes down vertically, bisecting it and creating a cross. You see, even our scars can be redeemed!

Can we dare to believe that brokenness can be beautiful, even in ourselves? There's a story I love that brings this home.

A water bearer in China had to travel several miles each day to get water for his master's garden. Two pots hung either side of his shoulders on each end of a pole. One of the pots had a crack in it and leaked, while the other was perfect and didn't lose a drop.

For two whole years, the man would arrive back at his master's house with just one and a half pots of water, the other half having been lost. The perfect pot delighted in its perfect performance, feeling proud of what it had achieved, while the cracked pot just became sad, ashamed of its brokenness.

After two years of this apparent failure, the cracked pot spoke to the water bearer by the stream.

'I want to apologise,' it said, 'for the time and effort I've wasted.'

'What do you mean?' asked the water bearer.

'Well, for the past two years, I've only been able to deliver half the water because of my brokenness. I leak water all the way home so you don't get what you should for your efforts.'

The water bearer felt sorry for the old cracked pot and said, 'I want you to notice and enjoy the beautiful flowers along the path on the way home.'

The pot enjoyed the journey home, with the sun shining down and the flowers on the path, but it was still sad by the time they arrived as it had again lost half its load. It apologised again for its failure.

The bearer then said to the pot, 'Did you notice that there were only flowers on one side of the path? That's because I've always known about your flaw and sought to make the most of it. So I planted flower seeds along your side of the road and let you water them as we walked. And all this time, I've been able to pick them and decorate my master's table. Without you being the way you are, he wouldn't have such beautiful flowers in his home.'

At the end of the day, we're all cracked pots. But, luckily for us, that's God's speciality.

Calling

The author Mark Twain said, 'The two most important days in your life are the day you are born and the day you find out why.' And yet finding out the *why* can be the hardest thing to do … How do we make the most of what we've been given? How do you find out what your calling is? And by that, I mean what we're made to do.

When it comes to thinking about calling, I find these words of Aristotle's to be really helpful: 'Where your talents and the world's needs cross, there lies your vocation.' There's wisdom in that. I mean, it's Aristotle after all! Boy, does the world have needs. But, goodness me, how talented we all are!

One of the richest seams of Christian belief and theology is the simple truth that we are all made in the 'image of God'. What this means is that there is something inherently good and noble about each one of us, something that reflects and speaks of God Himself, even in our mess and brokenness.

The amazing truth is that there has never been anyone quite like you, with your particular shape and make-up. Just as no single snowflake is like another, there neither has been, nor ever will be, another you. God made you unique, with all your strengths, creativity and talents!

So how do we make the most of what we've been given? How do you find out what your calling is?

Ask yourself this: what brings you most alive? When you're in a good place, feeling at peace and looking outward, not inward, what resonates most in your heart? And what do you have the skills to go and do? Because passion isn't enough, we need the competence to do it too. I enjoy playing tennis, but anyone who's seen me play wouldn't be entering me for Wimbledon!

As the world continues to open up and become more and more connected, and one decision now can seem as though it will open or close doors further down the line, it can leave us paralysed by the seemingly endless choices that we face. Perhaps because of this, many people are increasingly open to the idea of unseen forces leading and guiding us. You often hear the expression 'thank you universe' from people when something good has happened to them. But what if you could go one step further? What if it was possible to connect with the creator of this wondrous universe? The one who made us. The one who knows us. And the one who can tell us why we're here and the unique purpose of our life.

God is the Captain. He's the General. He'll deploy us where he wants. He'll put us where we're meant to be. He'll release us into a life that will truly make best use of our gifts and passions, where we'll truly feel alive. But it all flows from relationship. So, if you'd like to know your calling, come to the Director of it all. I never thought I'd end up as a vicar. For a long time I resisted it, convinced there would be nothing I'd enjoy less. But looking back, I can see how God knew what was best for me. A passion for God's word and spreading the good news, plus a love for people, meant that he knew the best fit for my gifts and personality.

You see, that's one of the great blessings of living a life of faith. It's simply the outworking of there being a God. Because if he was bothered enough to make us, and loved us enough to die for us, then he must certainly be interested in our lives and have things for us to do, a calling for us to pursue.

The stunning message of scripture is that there is no one quite like you, or me. We are unique. And we are uniquely loved. Indeed, before the creation of the world, God had us in mind and saw our days, our life, our shape. He has such amazing plans for us! He couldn't be more interested in you and your life and destiny.

Why hasn't it been plain sailing then, I hear you ask? Why have there been so many disappointments, so many wrong turns, so much grief and heartache? Well, the world isn't quite what it should be and, let's be honest, neither are we. We often know the good we should do, but somehow, time and again, we seem to put it off or do the opposite. It's as if there's a power at work within us that looks to sabotage our best intentions or divert us from our course.

But you see, that's why Jesus came. Before anything else existed, the Father, Son and Spirit desired that all should be redeemed, that all should be made new. That was Jesus' purpose in coming. That was his mission and calling. What looked like ending in failure, on a cross, was actually creating the path to our redemption, hope and future, for all things to be made new.

When Jesus walked the earth, other possibilities opened up, distractions and temptations came his way. The devil offered Jesus fame, glory, power, if he'd just worship him instead of God. But Jesus resisted. Why? Because he had each of us in mind. He didn't once lose his focus. And because of that, he fulfilled his purpose, stayed true to his calling, and was able to cry out 'it is finished' with his last breath upon the cross (John 19:30).

It sounds too good to be true, doesn't it? Like some sort of fairy tale. And yet it's rooted in history, and the claim is that it's true. And when you come into contact with this God, prepare for your life to change. And all for the better! Because he'll make you more truly yourself than you could ever have imagined. And he'll lead you into the things that he's uniquely called you to do.

There's a proverb I love that says, 'Trust in the Lord with all your heart and lean not on your own understanding; in all your ways submit to him, and he will make your paths straight' (Proverbs 3:5–6).

A life of faith enables you to let go of doubt and fear and take hold of hope instead. So when it comes to your future, let love be the lens for your decisions, the good of others the guideline for your choices. Therein lies the path to your calling and a life of abundance and purpose.

Only your maker knows the purpose for which he made you. So just reach out and ask him why. Or in the words of Saint Catherine of Siena, 'Be who God made you to be and you will set the world on fire.'

Courage

Why do we love films where there's such a clear line between good and evil? Where the underdog rises to achieve feats no one thought possible, overcoming the oppressor in a remarkable show of courage. Whether it's *Braveheart* (going back a bit here ... and a tad awkward as I'm English), *Gladiator*, *The Lord of the Rings* or *Star Wars*, we all love a story where true courage and valour are required and displayed in equal measure.

Could it be that we enjoy such tales because we know they're true to life? That we know we live in a world with plenty of shades of grey, but lots of light and darkness too? And our hearts rise at the thought of playing a part in creating a better world, at being part of a story that ends in hope instead of despair, success instead of defeat, life instead of death? I know I do. And the common currency to all these sagas? Courage. Something the dictionary describes as 'the ability to do something that frightens you'.

Whatever your station in life, whatever your background, education or means, wherever you find yourself in the world, and whomsoever you find yourself with when there, you are going to need courage!

We live in an increasingly divided, dissatisfied and dangerous world. Whether it's physical threats, both on an individual and national scale, or verbal assaults, threatening freedom of speech and expression, it seems that everything's getting more fraught with time, the marketplace of ideas more polarised. Simply standing your ground in this landscape, staying true to your values and principles, takes extraordinary courage.

Now, there are some who naturally seem to possess more of this virtue than others, but is there a way for us all to have more of it too? How do we tap this precious resource?

One of the most famous stories in the Bible is that of the battle between David and Goliath. It's the classic underdog story. David is an Israelite, from the people of God, and Goliath is a Philistine, one of the enemies of Israel. The Israelites and the Philistines are at war. Every day, for 40 days, this giant Goliath – who was around nine feet tall and armoured to the max – would come to the frontline and shout at the Israelites, challenging one of them to come and fight him in a winner-takes-all battle. But no one fancied it. Not one of the hardened, experienced warriors in Israel wanted to face off against the giant Goliath.

That is, none but David. He was a teenager, perhaps as young as 15, but when he heard Goliath's taunts, he felt affronted. In fact, he got personal, asking, 'Who is this uncircumcised Philistine that he should defy the armies of the living God?' (1 Samuel 17:26). David goes out to challenge Goliath, armed only with a sling and a few stones. I mean, talk about courage. That or foolishness! Goliath can't believe it, mocks him (as you would) and threatens to feed his flesh to the birds and wild animals. Lovely.

How would you feel in David's shoes? Or perhaps how *do* you feel? Are there things in your life right now that are downright terrifying, raising their voice and casting their shadow, seeking to keep you down or intimidate you? Health fears, financial worries, relational struggles, anxiety about the future or opposition from or conflict with people? How do you find the courage to stand up to that, or them, or whatever it may be?

How did David? Well, he tells us: 'You come against me with sword and spear and javelin, but I come against you in the name of the Lord Almighty, the God of the armies of Israel, whom you have defied. This day the Lord will deliver you into my hands, and I'll strike you down and cut off your head' (1 Samuel 17:45–46). (Again, lovely, but I guess that's just how they spoke.) And the rest, as they say, is history. David took Goliath down with a sling and a stone and then went up and cut off his head.

Impressive. But how did David *really* win this battle? Where did he find his courage? He found it through faith in his God, under whose name he went out to fight Goliath.

You see, that's the difference that faith can make. Faith lets you know you're never alone. It gives you courage when you most need it. It allows you to pick fights you should never win. Because it connects you with God, who's there and longs to be in your camp.

I remember a time in my own life when I was running from an event in my past – something that threatened to overwhelm me and that I seemed to have no answers for. The voices would come saying, 'Who do you think you are?', 'You'll never be free, you can never change.' One day, when I'd been a Christian for seven or eight years, those voices came knocking once more. But this time, I'd had enough. So in my heart, instead of running, I turned and faced my enemy. For once I stood my

ground and told that bully, 'enough is enough'. I declared who I was – a child of God who's been set free – and commanded that lying voice to be gone. And do you know what, it worked! I felt a breakthrough in my spirit, a real shift deep down within me. There've been skirmishes since, but the stronghold has been broken. And it can be the same for you as well.

As the great President Theodore Roosevelt put it, 'The credit belongs to the man who is actually in the arena, whose face is marred by dust and sweat and blood; who strives valiantly … and who at the worst, if he fails, at least fails while daring greatly.'

So go out and pick some fights! (Unless they're physical ones, in which case, don't!)

Creativity

There's an expression that's appeared in the last few years that perhaps you've noticed too. It might even be one you use. It's 'I'm a creative'. Now, on one level, I'm all for it. It immediately communicates something fundamental about that person, their priorities and approach to life. I get it. But on another level, I really don't like it, because it seems to suggest that the world is divided into those who are creative and those who aren't; those who express themselves authentically and those who possibly do so less.

Now, while we can all agree that there are some who are disproportionately talented and skilled at creating things – whether it be art or music or film, painting or dance or whatever – and who go on to make a living from it, to suggest that those of us who are left behind to fill the pews of accountancy practices, law firms, insurance brokerages or even churches are not is to miss something fundamental about our humanity.

To Christians, the simple truth of it is that we are all incredibly and unavoidably creative because we're all made in the image of God, and the first thing we learn about that God, according to Genesis, the first book of the Bible, is that God is creative. He created ... everything! From the vastness of the universe to the cuteness of the hedgehog. From the Northern lights and mountains to the African plains and seas. Creativity … it's literally the first thing we're told about God's nature. Before we learn of his power, or glory, or holiness, or love, we learn that he's creative. And we learn that we're made in his image.

Which means to say, whether you feel it or not, whether you like it or not, you are fundamentally creative too. It's in your make-up, your DNA. It's who you are at your deepest level. The fact that you might not be able to draw in a straight line, sing a note in tune, string a poetic sentence together or move your body in time to a beat is completely and utterly irrelevant. That just means your gifts may lie elsewhere. In how you think, in how you speak, in how you see the world, and in how you would do any and all of those things anyway. Sure, you might not win any prizes, but expressing yourself in any one of those mediums, or the hundreds of others available, is you being creative, is you exercising your God-given birthright and nature.

I was never particularly good at art, although I somehow managed to get an A in my GCSE, although that might have had something to do with me submitting two or three still-life watercolour offcuts from my good friend Nick Devereux who went on to become a professional artist. (Yes, that's something of a confession. Forgive me, board of examiners, it was in my pre-Christian days!) But I remember going on a date to a place that laid on a delicious dinner followed by a life drawing session. It was run by two sisters, friends of mine, one of whom was the chef, the other the artist. We finished our food and were then handed a piece of charcoal and a big sheet of paper. A naked woman stood before us – it was very Renaissance! – and we set about sketching her: drawing the outlines, wrestling with perspective and ratio, then smudging bits to get that charcoal effect. Now, as much as I've tried to claim that there was something rather Gustav Klimt about my work – the pose, the shape, the certain *je ne sais quoi* – I have since had to admit that what I actually produced was an over-elongated cartoon figure with a pea-sized head.

But that's all irrelevant, because my point is this: while it may not hang in the National Portrait Gallery (yet), it did something in me that took me quite by surprise. It released an energy, joy and engagement that I'd just not had before. The very creative act itself – the use of my mind, imagination and body – felt hugely therapeutic and released a desire for more. However poor the eventual outcome, the very act felt right and good.

And it's never too late to start. A friend of mine only last week spent a night painting Warhammer figures with a friend (yes, the tiny soldiers) – the first time he'd done so for 25 years. I asked him how he found it and he replied, 'Actually, I really loved it. It's so cool to distil your world to one tiny thing and focus on it for hours. Funnily enough, I find it really centring. Last year I also tried life drawing. Once I got past the naked bloke, it quickly became somebody, literally. After a while, I got quite lost in the process and overcame a bunch of my issues with art and ability, especially when compared with my artist father.'

Another mate of mine's father, in his mid-eighties, broke his neck in a car crash, from which he mainly recovered, but he could no longer pursue his first love of kayaking. So he took up model trains, which he'd loved as a boy, and is now part of a train enthusiast group with a bunch of other older men. Through it, he's been able to reconnect with his childhood, which was very painful, and now finds redemption in his hobby.

And a university friend's mother was told at school that she was dreadful at art. Then, after she retired and moved to France, a friend offered to teach her to paint in return for English lessons and she found she has a real gift that has given her endless joy. That same friend's father retired from over 40 years in the army and took up dressmaking (yes, you heard that correctly). He has now turned my friend's sister's old bedroom into a sewing room and the whole family have various items of clothing that he has made.

Let me say it again, we are all creative! It's just a matter of getting out there and discovering just how.

So stare down the naysayers. Shut up that voice of doubt, or comparison, that voice from the past, and go and run that race, sing that song, paint that picture and dance like no one's watching (if you're really that bad, they probably won't be anyway!).

Destiny

I love films. I especially love ones that speak about destiny and hope, or the battle of good and evil. Isn't it interesting, though, that all the greatest stories seem to share the same themes: light/darkness, good/evil, freedom/captivity, life/death? What if that's because there's an overarching story going on, to which these lesser ones bear echo ...? What if there's a story being played out in which we all can have a role? What if the choices we make determine the ultimate ending of our life? As the great Chinese philosopher Lao Tzu said, 'Watch your thoughts, they become your words. Watch your words, they become your actions. Watch your actions, they become your habits. Watch your habits, they become your character. Watch your character, it becomes your destiny.'

Do we have a destiny? Yes, I believe we do. Indeed, the Bible tells us that, 'All the days ordained for me were written in your book before one of them came to be' (Psalm 139:16). Our lives have purpose and meaning – you were created to walk in them.

But how would you even discover your destiny? Well, with this conversation, we're now in the land of faith and spirituality, of the invisible and supernatural. Because to even say the word is to admit that there's more to this world than meets the eye.

That there are forces and powers we cannot see. That somehow, somewhere, something or someone is pulling the strings.

So, are we just pawns in a cosmic game of chess? Well, yes and no. Yes, in that such a being must be of incomparable power and so can use us how they please. But no, in that this creator has clearly given us free will and so we're able to make free choices. In this sense, destiny should not be confused with fate, which is a different concept altogether that suggests we've no freedom to avoid what's coming. Rather, the Judeo-Christian tradition has always held that we're autonomous beings with the very real burden of responsibility and choice. In this regard, we can truly partner with God and trust in him to lead us on. In other words, we're more than just a rain drop whose destiny is shaped by the wind!

The Continental Divide of the Americas is the name given to the largely mountainous hydrological divide that separates the watersheds that drain into the Pacific Ocean from those that drain into the Atlantic. It starts in Alaska, then runs through Canada, the centre of the US, Mexico and down through South America. They say that a house situated on top of this Divide can determine whether a drop of rainfall will end up in the Pacific or the Atlantic. A fraction of an inch can make the difference, depending on where it hits the peak of the roof.

Part of what brought me to faith was recognising that there's just too much beauty and wonder and magic in the universe for there to be nothing more behind it. So, if there is such a being, then it would stand to reason that to truly know our destiny, we must first come to him.

A life of faith means recognising that we were made for eternity and our lives on earth will echo in it. So many people go through life never truly discovering their purpose or destiny.

They never came to God to ask him!

When Jesus walked this earth, he knew his purpose. Part of it was to build a family of believers, create a community and establish a church. This all began as he walked along the shore of the Sea of Galilee. He saw a man called Simon, whom he later christened Peter, fishing with his brother Andrew. He called them both to follow him and said he'd make them fishers of men. (Truth be told, they weren't great fishermen anyway, especially Peter it would seem, so they didn't have much to lose!)

I've always loved Jesus' relationship with Peter. There's something so real and encouraging about it, probably because Peter makes so many mistakes but Jesus just keeps on loving and welcoming him back. But alongside this, he clearly saw in Peter the heart of a leader, something Peter struggled to see in himself. He nurtured him, trained him up and even called him 'the rock' on which he'd build his church. Peter went on to become the leader of the early church. And one day, on the day of Pentecost, when the Holy Spirit was poured out, Peter preached the gospel, let down spiritual nets for a catch and saw thousands come to faith!

Could he have imagined that three and a half years earlier? No! Did his destiny change when Jesus called him? Yes! He never thought he'd go on to lead the life he led as he went about his fishing … But Jesus knew. He could see. And he led him to fulfil his destiny.

God knows we're wrestling with these big questions. But sometimes we must just 'be' and let the answer come to us. That's what happened to Peter. And it can happen to you and me as well, if we'll only let it …

Eternity

There are many things in life that I just can't get my head round. One of them is eternity. I mean, the idea of things going on forever and ever and ever ... it's just crazy, right? I've been alive for just four decades, and that seems long enough!

We get a glimpse of the concept of eternity when we contemplate the universe and how long it's been around – some 13.8 billion years. And yet here we are, a goosebump on a planet going round a star – a mere blip in history. However, if the scriptures are to be believed, we are part of some cosmic plan and design that reveals the very glory of God.

Yes, I know not many of us are that keen on the idea of life as we know it going on forever, as we're all familiar with suffering and pain, with heartache and disappointment. (Not to mention gammy knees, sore backs or weak bladders ...)

But that's not what's on offer in Christianity. Instead, through faith, a different future opens up. One of imperishable bodies, that won't age or decay, in a perfected, new creation. Let me get one thing clear: what Christians believe is almost unbelievable! It sounds like a fairy tale with icing and a cherry on top to boot. So how can we take it seriously? Well, one word, or one claim: the resurrection. Because if that bit is true, then it all is, while if that didn't happen, then we're wasting our time.

I am personally convinced that the resurrection *did* happen. And that, because of it, the very life of God, who is eternal, is opened up to us. Can you imagine how beautiful and glorious he must be – the creator of the mountains and the skies, the sun, moon and stars, the rivers and oceans and trees? I promise you one thing, eternity with him won't be boring!

And what's funny to me is that we all seem to long for it. Be it at moments of greatest joy, like the birth of a child, or moments of greatest sadness, like the loss of a loved one. There seems to be something in the human heart that just knows we were made for more …

Having faith doesn't so much change the experiences we have as give us a different lens to see them through. When you believe there's an author of life, you begin to look for evidence of their guidance and handiwork. The Bible says, '"What no eye has seen, what no ear has heard, and what no human mind has conceived" – the things God has prepared for those who love him' (1 Corinthians 2:9). And it's good … it's so, so good.

Don't project forward from your current feelings or circumstances, the fact that you may not be happy right now; that's not the lens to look at eternity through. Indeed, the correct lens hasn't even been revealed. But suffice it to say, it will all be new … and we'll be fitted out to enjoy it forever! As C. S. Lewis once said, 'As we grow older, we become like old cars – more and more repairs and replacements are necessary. We must just look forward to the fine new machines (latest resurrection model) which are waiting for us, we hope, in the Divine garage.'

Well, I want to assure you that, for all who trust in Jesus, those models are waiting. This is why they call it 'Good News'! There's a story I love that demonstrates this. A young boy fell down a flight of stairs and shattered his back. As a result, he spent most of his childhood and teenage years in and out of hospital. The former Bishop of Maidstone, Gavin Read, spoke to him in church:

> Gavin asked, 'How old are you?'
> 'Seventeen,' the boy replied.
> 'How many years have you spent in and out of hospital?'
> The boy answered, 'Thirteen.'
> Gavin asked, 'Do you think that is fair?'
> He replied, 'God has got all of eternity to make it up to me.'

Imagine the time when you felt most alive, when your soul and body were as one – the highest high, the happiest moment. Maybe when you fell in love, or climbed a mountain, or went on holiday, or just got into bed when you were exhausted! Now imagine every cell in your body attuned to the very life and glory of God, every part of you buzzing, feeling alive and radiating light – more beautiful than the most stunning person or creature depicted in art or film! That's what's on offer. That's the Christian understanding of the life to come.

No floating around on a cloud business. No need to learn the harp. The new age of eternity will be real, embodied, singing and dancing for joy. Everything made new! Everything you ever hoped for or dreamt of. The party that never ends, with new wine that never runs out. Sharing the very life and happiness of God. This is what's on offer and everyone is invited.

And you know what, it's not even something you need to wait for, because that life can begin right now, as you connect with your creator and God's new age breaks in on ours. He brings heaven to earth, new life to what's dead, where our spirit comes alive. Heaven is described as a feast, like a party, but the foot-tapping can start down here, as we hear the beat of its drum draw near.

Failure

~

I questioned whether to even include this entry – my natural inclination is to keep things positive and uplifting, but I just felt this had to be in here. Why? Because all of us face failure and will experience it at some point in our lives. Failure is just part of life. In fact, it's impossible to try anything new or attempt any great project without experiencing failure. As Albert Einstein said, 'A person who never made a mistake never tried anything new.'

Rather, I think it should be mandatory for schools to teach a whole term on why failure is an admirable and marvellous thing (when you've done your best and prepared as well as you could have). Schools should teach pupils that failure doesn't need to spell the end and how, if you persevere when you think something is right, you may see the tables turned.

But then again, you may well not. Because sometimes we just lose, we fail, we come up that little bit short, and we don't get another chance – be it in sport, or business, or relationships, or any area of life for that matter. The threat of failure hovers like an ever-present spectre, trying to intimidate us out of even trying. But we must! Because where would we be if we just gave in? Instead, let us have the same resolve as the great Winston

Churchill (and he experienced more than his fair share of failure, despite appearances), who said: 'Success is the ability to go from one failure to another with no loss of enthusiasm'.

And it's always worth keeping in mind that other failures may just be temporary. Even people who are remembered as the greatest failed: the Beatles were rejected by four respected recording companies; Walt Disney was fired by a newspaper editor for lack of ideas; Isaac Newton did very badly at school; Beethoven was called hopeless as a composer by his teacher; J. K. Rowling was rejected by 12 different publishing houses before Bloomsbury agreed to bring Harry Potter to the wider world; Henry Ford failed and went broke five times before he finally succeeded; Marilyn Monroe's first contract with Columbia Pictures expired in 1948 before she'd even acted in a movie; and Thomas Edison failed 1,000 times before success-fully inventing the prototype of the light bulb. Are you feeling encouraged yet? Well, here's one more for you: they crucified Jesus Christ on Good Friday, but then three days later ...

Now, in one sense, all life ends in failure and defeat, because one out of one of us dies, which aren't great odds, let's be honest. But I have one word for that: resurrection. The unique selling point of the Christian faith comes into its own at this precise moment. For the Bible tells us that even death – man's greatest enemy and ultimate proof of our failure, if you will – has been undone and disarmed. As Paul puts it, quoting the prophet Hosea, 'Where, O death, is your victory? Where, O death, is your sting?' (1 Corinthians 15:55).

For when you live under grace, from a place of security and unconditional acceptance, you find the courage to take those risks, knowing that any failure won't be 'fatal' and that resurrection and redemption are on their way. So in a very real sense, you can't lose, even when you lose. Or as my friend Disni said, a few days before passing away from cancer just 30 days after her diagnosis, 'It's a win–win situation Pat: either God heals me and I get to serve him longer on Earth, or he doesn't and I go to be with him in heaven.'

Faith

I've lost track of the number of people who've said to me over the years, 'I wish I could believe, but I can't' or, 'I wish I had your faith.' I know exactly what they mean. It's tempting to think that faith is something you either have or don't have. That it's like a gene that you're either born with or without. Like brown hair or blue eyes. And it can often look that way. Where I try to encourage such people and gently push back is through saying that rather than being a gene that some are born with but others aren't, faith is more akin to a muscle that needs to be worked out or a story that needs to be lived in.

If you think about it, we're all living out of one story or another: that we're loved or that we're not; that people are good or that they're bad; that the universe has meaning or that it's random; that there's a God or that there's nothing. And whatever story we accept as true will influence how we live and the choices we make. But whatever story we live by, we all exercise faith to dwell within it. So, all I say to people who are searching now is, why not give living in the Christian story a go for six months or a year? Go to church, pray, sing the hymns and worship songs, read the Bible, give generously and love your neighbour, then see how you feel after that.

Because faith can be learnt, it can be taught, it can be caught. But it must also be acted upon because, as James tells us in his letter, 'faith by itself, if it is not accompanied by action, is dead' (James 2:17). What does such action look like? Well, more often than not, it looks like getting up off our backsides, moving out of our comfort zone and taking an actual step of faith, perhaps not knowing where it may lead.

One such example in my own life came shortly after the attempted assassination of the ex-Russian spy, Sergei Skripal, in Salisbury.

It was my day off and I'd decided to go and visit my mother in Hampshire. I was chilling at home, watching Sky Sports or something, when a news update popped up giving us the latest about Sergei and his daughter Yulia, as well as Detective Sergeant Nick Bailey, who had all been infected by the Novichok poison left on their door handle.

And it suddenly struck me ... they were being treated in Salisbury District Hospital just 10 minutes down the road from where I was! And the following thought came into my head, 'Go and pray for them.' Now, one of the trickier things for Christians is working out what might be God speaking and what might be just our own ideas or imagination after eating too much cheese. Well, I hadn't had any cheese that day and when I tried to dismiss the idea, it just came back again.

My immediate response was, 'Come on Lord, what a ridiculous idea. I won't be able to get near them! The security, the doctors, it would be a complete waste of time ...'

But that gentle whisper persisted, saying, 'Go and pray for them.'

So I began to get organised. I didn't have my 'dog collar' with me; not ideal, I thought, but at least I'm dressed in black, wearing jeans and my black bomber jacket. So I sort of looked priestly.

What else would I need? Well, I'll need some anointing oil to pray for them with, if by some miracle I get to see them. But obviously I didn't have any of that with me, so I grabbed a tiny inch-cubed Tupperware pot from the kitchen and filled it with some olive oil.

I then jumped in my car and headed off to the hospital. I parked up, made my way through a side entrance, didn't speak to anyone and headed up to intensive care on the fourth floor, where I proceeded to run out of ideas and just wandered around, looking ever so slightly dodgy, unshaven and dressed in black.

I didn't know where to find them exactly, so I went up to a couple of medical staff, a nurse and then a porter, saying, 'So sorry, but I don't suppose you can help me? I'm looking for the Skripals. Do you know where I might find them? I'm a vicar in the Church of England you see and I'd really like to pray for them.'

As you can imagine, I didn't get very far and was given short shrift. I lingered by the intensive care doors, but you have to buzz and get permission to go in, so that didn't work either. I contemplated ghosting in behind a patient on a bed at one point, but thought better of that, too.

In the end, I just had to resign myself to the fact that I wasn't going to get near them, as I'd suspected and told the Lord, so I gave up and sat down on a windowsill. Instead, I decided to spend a few minutes praying for them, asking God's blessing on them, praying for his healing and that this wouldn't end in death, but instead would end in life.

I did that for a bit, as a security guard walking nonchalantly passed, then headed out and drove home, thinking no more about it.

Three days later, in London, the vicarage doorbell rang. I went and opened the door and was greeted by two women dressed in normal clothes, or I should say 'plain clothes', because they were policewomen! A friend who knows about these things reckons they were possibly even MI5 or MI6 to have had clearance for that case, but who knows.

They said hello, flashed a badge of some sort, asked if I was Patrick Allerton and then requested if they could come in. I said no and shut the door. I'm joking – of course I said yes, checking first that no one had died! It's very unrelaxing having the police turn up on your doorstep. They said all was fine but that they wanted to ask me a few questions.

The first was, 'Is it right that I'd been in Salisbury recently?' I said yes.

They then asked, 'Did you visit the hospital while you were there?' 'Yesss,' I replied, suddenly knowing where this was heading.

'And is it right you were looking for the Skripals while there? Are you family friends with the Skripals?'

'No,' I answered, suddenly feeling slightly under the cosh, 'but I'm a vicar in the Church of England and I just felt called to go and pray for them.'

Slight pause from them, before they asked, 'Have you got any proof that you're a vicar?' Cue desperate searching of the house for any documents or photographs that might show that I'm legit. In the end I had to resort to Facebook and a photo of me in clerical robes, officiating a friend's wedding. Fortunately, I think they believed me.

I had to give a full police statement lasting 45 minutes and even make myself available for any court date, should the need arise.

Almost arrested, or so it felt, for going to pray for some people!

I did later reflect that it probably wasn't the wisest idea to turn up unannounced at a hospital, asking for the Skripals, dressed like an assassin, holding a small pot of unidentified liquid … But I would do it all over again, because my heart's desire that day was for life to be their story and for God's healing to reach them. Thank goodness they all recovered.

My point is this: faith always looks like something. And it's often spelt R–I–S–K.

One of my favourite images of 'faith' comes in *Indiana Jones and the Last Crusade*. Perhaps you remember the scene … Indiana is faced with an apparent chasm and no ability to jump the gap, but the evidence points to taking a step of faith. So that's exactly what he does and, as he steps out, his foot lands on a stone bridge that had simply been disguised from his sight before then. Faith isn't irrational. It doesn't require you to check your brain in at the door. Indeed, some of the biggest 'brains' in history have been Christians! Rather, it's reasonable, it's based in history and it transforms life here and now. But it does require a step, some buy-in, an RSVP to the invite. Indiana Jones took that step, and he found the 'Holy Grail'. Nothing less is on offer to you.

So how about you start doubting your doubts and believing your beliefs? You never know where it might lead. Because it's a story to be lived in, a muscle to be flexed. And you can take your first step of faith right now, knowing God is there to catch you if you fall.

Fear

We live in extraordinary times. It's a strange reality to hold together in one's mind, the feeling that anything is possible and there's no limit to what we can achieve, to then thinking we're five minutes away from disaster and that the world's about to end. Be it climate change or World War III, mental health issues or social media saturation. I don't know what it is, but life seems rather overwhelming! No wonder the data shows an exponential increase in depression and anxiety in recent years. It feels like we're being pushed to breaking point and we can often feel out of control.

I think this is the primary sort of fear I'm talking about. Not so much the fear of speaking in public or fear when swimming in the sea and your mind tells you there's a shark (the annoying thing with that one is we'll never really know!). No, I think the most prevalent fear for us all is a sense of things being out of control and not knowing what the future holds in such a fast-changing world. That, and our own mortality.

It was interesting to see how anxious and fearful people became during the Covid-19 pandemic. And for understandable reasons. In those early days particularly, when there was no vaccine and we understood less, a spectre of sickness and death stalked the streets and dominated the headlines. You couldn't pick up a paper (hard to even get one when locked indoors!) or turn on the TV without seeing headlines detailing how many infections and how many deaths had occurred that day.

And I guess that's the ultimate fear isn't it, from which all the others take their cue, be it the end of a relationship, loss of financial security, health worries or climate concerns. They're all shadows, to one degree or another, of our real and greatest enemy and fear: death. Death operates in the shadows, ever-present, lurking in the back of our minds. We pretend it's not there, kick the can down the road and try to ignore it all together.

Comedian Russell Brand once said that 'laughter is addictive because ... it gives us a temporary escape – for the moment it stops the fear of the inevitability of death.' Strong words, but isn't it true? We do our best to distract ourselves so we're too busy to face our own fragile mortality, or we refer to death euphemistically. I even heard about a hospital that began referring to death as 'negative patient care outcome'. Well, that's one way of putting it! But whichever way we spin it, people die and we lose the ones we love.

Which is why I'm really not a fan of a popular funeral poem by Henry Scott Holland that goes:

Death is nothing at all.
It does not count.
I have only slipped away into the next room.
Nothing has happened.

Everything remains exactly as it was.
I am I, and you are you,

and the old life that we lived so fondly together is untouched, unchanged.

Whatever we were to each other, that we are still.

I simply think it isn't true. Death *is* something. Something really *has* happened, even for Christians: the life we knew has changed forever and they're sadly not in the next-door room: if only.

Now don't get me wrong, I really hear the heart of this poem and admire the fight for hope that's found within it. But a hope that's not true is no hope at all. It's like a doctor telling a terminally ill patient that they're fine just so they don't hurt their feelings. But that's the whole point! Death is real, and it hurts, and it robs and it steals from every single one of us. It's an enemy, not a friend. No wonder we fear it like we do.

But here's the thing – and this is the crux of why faith changes everything – Jesus came to make enemies, friends. He came to bring light to the darkness, hope to the hopeless, and life where there'd been death. And it's because of his resurrection that the grave is empty, death really is defeated, that we can truly find hope and know our deepest fear, and all its pals, driven out. Because of the promise of God, we can turn and face our fears and look them in the eye and say, 'you're done, get out of here'. A life of faith brings fearless living, where that great enemy can become a friend as it's the gateway to life with God.

In an interview with Nicky Gumbel in 2009, he talks about how Mother Teresa was once asked shortly before her death, 'Are you afraid of dying?' She replied, 'How can I be? Dying is going home to God. I've never been afraid. No. On the contrary, I'm really looking forward to it!'

Can you say the same? Because here's the truth: until you

can, you'll never know true peace or freedom. You'll always live with nagging fear. Because that final frontier awaits us, and we must all soon pass its way.

Up until the fifteenth century, no one in Europe knew whether it was possible to sail past South Africa, around the bottom of the Cape. For them it was the edge of the map, the bottom of the world. Europeans called it the 'Cape of Storms', because the storms were so bad that every ship that had ever tried to sail around the Cape either turned around and came back, or was shipwrecked.

And so people speculated about whether it was possible to navigate, and what they might find on the other side, because nobody knew. Some said maybe there's something, others suggested that there was nothing, and that if you went too far, you'd simply drop off the map into the great abyss. No one knew for certain. Until Vasco da Gama, the Portuguese explorer, successfully sailed around the Cape of Storms in 1497, making it all the way to India.

How do we know he got to the other side? Because he came back, and he proved you don't just drop off the map into nothing. He had spices from India to prove it! And so they renamed it. It's no longer the Cape of Storms; instead it's called the 'Cape of Good Hope'.

And death is like that for those who believe. None of us knows what's on the other side of death because we haven't been there. The only way we could possibly know is if someone went there and came back, and that's exactly what Jesus did. At least that's what Christianity claims.

And all I can say, having been a believer for 25 years, is that I've known a lot less fear than before and there's nothing in life or death that can scare me now. And it can be the same for you.

Forgiveness

All of us, everywhere, at some point in our life, will have someone we need to forgive. We may not like it, we probably won't feel like doing it, but the simple truth is that if we don't, then it will be us who suffer. Nelson Mandela described resentment as like 'drinking poison and then hoping it will kill your enemies'. We may think we're punishing them, but we're actually hurting ourselves.

The problem is that some of us are addicted to poison! Well, certainly in small enough quantities. It sometimes feels good to hold on, it feels right to go over things again and again. We think our anger and judgement can bring us a sense of control and vindication, somehow allowing us to hold on to lost relationships, people or situations. Rehearsing events in our minds can bring a sense of proximity to them. After all, aren't we right to feel deeply aggrieved, weren't we the ones to be wronged and betrayed? To forgive would dishonour myself, my loved one, the situation. It would say I don't care, that it was somehow all right, and it would allow that person to get off scot-free. So we can sometimes tell ourselves. Besides, how is forgiveness even possible if you just feel anger, hurt and loss?

There's an expression that goes, 'hurt people, hurt people'.

Meaning that until you're healed of your own wounds, you're likely to inflict them on others. Well, in the same way, you could say that 'forgiven people, forgive people'. This is what Jesus meant when he taught his disciples the Lord's Prayer, saying, 'Forgive us our sins, for we also forgive everyone who sins against us' (Luke 11:4). In other words, when you know you've been forgiven for all the bad stuff you've done, you're able to forgive others for what they do to you.

And here's the ridiculously good news: in Christ, God offers each one of us forgiveness for everything we've ever done wrong. Even that thing that comes to mind right now! Nothing is beyond his grace and mercy. All we have to do is bring it to him, and he'll take it off our shoulders. So many people go through life weighed down by guilt and shame. Not knowing what to do with it all. Not knowing how to be forgiven and make a fresh start. Well, the claim of Christianity is that Jesus is that fresh start. When he died on the cross, we read in the gospels that the curtain in the temple – which had previously separated God's dwelling place from ours, the holy from the unholy – was torn in two. The death of Jesus washes us clean! The partition has been removed.

Which means we can freely come to God. He'll forgive us and bring us home. You can be free of the past, free of guilt and shame. Free from whatever holds you back. And when you truly experience that, you find the strength to forgive others. Because you've now got God's resources to draw on. An endless well of 'living water' (think a spiritual source of satisfaction and life that just bubbles up within us, like a spring that won't run dry). So drink deep and pass it on …

We see this again and again in the gospels. When Jesus visited Jericho, he came across a man called Zacchaeus. He was a chief tax collector and was wealthy. His own people hated him because he was in cahoots with the Romans and was feathering his own nest at their expense, defrauding his own people. Jesus was passing through and Zacchaeus wanted to see him but couldn't because he was short. So he ran ahead and climbed a sycamore tree. When Jesus passed by, he called Zacchaeus by name and asked him to come down, because he wanted to stay at his house that day.

Over dinner later, Zacchaeus suddenly stood up and said, 'Look, Lord! Here and now I give half of my possessions to the poor, and if I have cheated anybody out of anything, I will pay back four times the amount' (Luke 19:8).

You see, the truth is that he'd been carrying a terrible sense of guilt and condemnation all that time, even though, deep down, he longed to be free from it. When Jesus showed up, chose him and showed him grace and love, it so softened and transformed him that he turned his life around and put things right.

This is the power that forgiveness can have in our lives too. When we turn to Christ, he connects us with God and we experience his loving embrace. When that happens, we find the strength to forgive other people, no matter what they've done.

Corrie ten Boom was an inspirational Dutch Christian who hid Jews from the Nazis during World War II. Along with her father and sister, she was caught and sent to concentration camps. Her father sadly died, as did her sister Betsie, who'd gone with her to Ravensbrück. Somehow, Corrie survived and spent the rest of her life going round the world, talking about the importance of forgiveness.

One time, at a church in Munich in 1947, a man she recognised as one of the guards from Ravensbrück came up to her after her talk.

He said to her, 'Thank you for your wonderful message about forgiveness. I have become a Christian, and I know that God has forgiven me. I want to know that you forgive me.'

And with that, he held out his hand and said, 'Shake my hand as a sign that you've forgiven me.'

But for Corrie, it all came flooding back – the memories of her dear sister dying, his cruelty in the camp – and she describes how she just couldn't shake his hand. Betsie had died there; did he think he could just undo that simply by asking for forgiveness? Although she recalls that it can't have been more than a few seconds that they stood there, facing one another, with his hand held out, she said it felt like hours as she wrestled with all these thoughts. All she felt was coldness in her heart. She prayed to the Lord to come and help her.

She writes in *The Hiding Place*:

… woodenly, mechanically, I thrust my hand into the one stretched out to me. And as I did, an incredible thing took place. The current started in my shoulder, raced down my arm, sprang into our joined hands, and then this healing warmth seemed to flood my whole being, bringing tears to my eyes.
'I forgive you, brother,' I cried, 'with all my heart.'
I have never known God's love so intensely as I did then.

This is a picture of what forgiveness truly looks like. It can release us all into a new future, filled with greater peace and love and hope. So let me ask you a simple question: is there anyone you need to forgive today …?

Freedom

There are few words more compelling or pregnant with a sense of hope and promise than 'freedom'. Books have been written about it, epic stories told, movies depict the battle for it, because, deep down, everybody wants it.

And yet, can anyone claim to really have it? Let me ask you a question: do you feel free? I don't mean physical freedom, or freedom to make your own decisions, go your own way or be your own person. I mean freedom deep down in your soul. Freedom from fear or worry or shame. Freedom from self-doubt or self-hatred or just plain selfishness. Freedom that comes from truly knowing you're free.

Hey, the truth is, no one on earth can say they feel that 100 per cent, all the time. That's just the human condition. Artists and philosophers have been wrestling to make sense of this reality down the ages. The political philosopher Jean-Jacques Rousseau said, 'Man was born free, and everywhere he is in chains', while Karl Marx holds out the theory of class struggle and the subordination of one group by another as evidence of a lack of freedom. But is our existential angst and wrestle really just the result of unjust societal structures and the selfish actions of others? Or is there some deeper power at play that inherently holds us back?

My dad has lots of big photograph frames on his walls, poster boards really, with photos from our childhood. So many memories. So much fun to look at them! But one of his favourite pictures of me is from when I'm about three or four and coming out of the sea, making a face, wearing a bright yellow T-shirt with the slogan, 'Here Comes Trouble'. And the reality is, that wasn't far from the truth. I was a handful – rebellious and inherently naughty from the start! And what's strange is that no one needed to teach me how to be like that – it just seemed innate. It all came so naturally to me! Sure, I probably imitated others, what I saw, but I also pioneered some of my own moves too. I didn't struggle for inspiration, which suggests there's something in our make-up – as I don't think I'm the only one – something inherent to human nature that veers away from God's standards. And if that's true, can I really be free?

There's a verse in Psalm 51 that helps explain this. It says, 'Surely I was sinful at birth, sinful from the time my mother conceived me' (Psalm 51:5). What this seems to say, and where it differs to Marx or Rousseau, is that the problem of a lack of freedom isn't just 'out there' (although it is, and we must fight for a more just and fair society), but rather, the root of the problem is 'in here', in our hearts, from the off.

The reason I mention all this is because it ultimately comes down to this: we will never be free if we're not truly free inside. You can be the richest person in the world, completely free on the outside, and yet feel totally trapped within yourself. God doesn't want that for you or me, which is why he came to set us free. The fullest meaning of salvation is freedom. God wants to set us free: free from guilt, free from shame, free from addiction, free from hopelessness.

I studied History of Art at school and was transfixed by the work of Michelangelo, the great Renaissance artist. His frescos on the Sistine Chapel ceiling are not only stunning art, but a superhuman effort, given that he had to do the whole thing while lying on his back. But he was also the most incredible sculptor. Perhaps his most famous piece is the 17-foot statue of David (of David and Goliath fame) that stands in the Accademia Gallery in Florence. It is remarkable. It looks so lifelike, it's hard to believe that it's carved out of solid marble. History records that Michelangelo brought David to life from a rejected slab of marble that had sat out in the elements for a quarter of a century. He would walk around the block of marble for hours, even days, until he could completely see David, trapped as it were, within the stone. When asked about his process and how he did it, he simply said that once he'd seen him clearly in the marble, he just 'chipped away all that wasn't David'.

I don't know about you, but I can sometimes feel a bit like David trapped within that slab of marble – rejected and forgotten about, wondering if the real me will ever be released. Well, Michelangelo's process is a kind of picture of how God deals with us. When you let him into your life, he lovingly gets to work. He looks, and he chips, and he shapes, and he polishes, until all that isn't us isn't there. Sometimes it hurts, sometimes we don't understand why we're going through things. But when we ultimately understand his heart, that he loves us and wants what's best for us, we can begin to go with and trust the process.

Freedom never comes cheaply – there's always a cost, there's always pain, but, in the end, it's always worth it. Because in Christ we can become who we were always made to be: God's masterpiece, for the display of his glory.

Now the problem many people have is that, far from seeing

God as someone who comes to bring us freedom, they see him as someone who comes to take it away. I'll never forget sharing that I was a Christian with a woman I'd just met at a party and her immediately saying, 'Remind me what that means you can't do.' She captured what so many people think. And yet what people forget is how generous and loving God is in the first place. I mean, let's keep in mind that he's given us this beautiful world richly to enjoy. That every gift and talent and good thing that we have comes from him. That he said to Adam and Eve at the start, 'You are free to eat from any tree in the garden; but you must not eat from the tree of the knowledge of good and evil' (Genesis 2:16–17). *Any* tree, bar one, in other words. Those are pretty good odds I'd say!

In a bid to define ourselves and make the rules, we end up losing contact with the overarching framework that provides set norms and practices to live by. In our quest for 'greater freedom', we lose sight of the parameters that guarantee it.

Imagine a game of football that has no lines, no fouls, not even any goals. You wouldn't know when the ball was out and you'd never know when a team had scored. Now you might be 'freer' in the technical sense of the term, but it wouldn't be football that you're playing.

A life of faith presents a different vision of a lasting path to freedom. One where you're transformed first on the inside, before seeking to transform the world around you. One where, instead of seeing 'rules', one sees guidelines that safeguard life and produce flourishing communities. One where, as the Book of Common Prayer puts it, we worship a God 'Whose service is perfect freedom'. That seems such a strange concept to us, doesn't it? That serving someone else should bring us freedom. And yet when it comes to the spiritual life, that's exactly what it brings. We all know the sense of fulfilment and satisfaction that comes from putting other people first. How is it that so often the most contented, joy-filled people in life aren't the rich and famous, but those who serve their fellow human beings?

'I have on my table a violin string,' wrote Bengali poet Rabindranath Tagore. 'If I twist one end, it responds; it is free. But it is not free to sing. So I fix it into my violin. I bind it and when it is bound, it is free for the first time to sing.'

True freedom can only be found in a life of self-renunciation and service of others, like the violin string that serves the ends of its master, achieving so much more than it would on its own. We all know this to be true. Whether it's volunteering with a local youth club or food bank, carrying out random acts of kindness or caring for children or elderly parents, we all know the sense of joy and fulfilment that serving others can bring. Indeed, the more we forget ourselves, the more we truly find ourselves. Theologians call it 'The upside-down kingdom', full of paradox and the unexpected. But it's as we learn to live this way that we find true freedom. The world's way, and whatever we have, will never seem enough.

There's a famous story about John D. Rockefeller, one of the richest men ever to have lived, being asked by a journalist, 'How much money is enough?' To which he responded, 'Just a little bit more.' Does that sound like freedom to you? No doubt Rockefeller had nice things, but, without contentment, what's the point?

Instead, offer your life to the one who knows best how to release all your potential and bring you lasting joy. And then just enjoy the ride.

Greatness

The Great Pyramid of Giza is the only surviving wonder of the ancient world. It is truly glorious to behold – vast in scale and even more impressive when you remember that it was built around 2500BC. But what really blew my mind was discovering that it is basically just a tomb – a burial site for one man, Pharaoh Khufu. I mean, how great do you need to be to get one of those as your resting place? I remember visiting a graveyard during my vicar training where they give families the option of burying their loved one vertically so they take up less space. Environmentally considerate, yes, but I'm not sure what Khufu would have made of it!

Greatness. From the beginning of time, man has strived for it – to reach the top, the pinnacle, the highest point of the pyramid. There's just something in our psyche that seems to crave it, wants a share of it. William Shakespeare said of greatness, 'Some are born great, some achieve greatness, and some have greatness thrust upon them.' We revere and celebrate those who achieve it, thus the contemporary 'celebrity' phenomenon, those who've climbed higher and further than us. But we have less time for those beneath us, whom we deem to be inferior. We crave the trappings of power and success, the doors it opens, the favour it brings, but shrink back from holding doors for others or doing favours when they cannot be returned. I sound a bit cynical, I know. Sorry, but it's true isn't it? We live in a world with a pyramid structure – where some people 'make it', but most people don't. There may be space for all at the bottom, but in this race to the top, it's elbows out. And we justify our actions and these structures in the name of achieving greatness. But at what cost? Is there not a fairer way to do it, where everyone can have a share?

One of the things I love about the Bible is its brutal honesty concerning all involved. There are no flawless heroes, no sinless characters. Moses, David, Peter ... all are shown to come up short. And when it comes to greatness, Jesus' disciples are no better than anyone else. There's a time when Jesus hears them arguing as they walk along the road. He later asks them what they were arguing about and they stay silent, embarrassed because they'd been arguing about who was the greatest among them. This happened on several occasions. In response, Jesus told them, 'whoever wants to become great among you must be your servant, and whoever wants to be first must be your slave – just as the Son of Man did not come to be served, but to serve, and to give his life as a ransom for many' (Matthew 20:25–28).

What I love about this is that Jesus flips the tables. He completely turns things on their head and inverts the world's way of doing things. And in so doing, he opens up greatness for all. Because all of us can serve, all of us can put others first, all of us can get 'lower' than our neighbour – be it helping someone with their weekly shop, picking up litter on the street, doing the washing up after a family meal or offering your seat to someone on a packed train. And in so doing, we will be like

Jesus, who did not come to be served, but to serve. I mean he washed his disciples' feet for goodness sake – covered in mud and crap and gunk! The Son of God, if indeed he is … what humility, what greatness. Truly the pyramid has been inverted and there's space for all who choose to go low. But instead of being forgotten about or left behind, as the world would have us believe, God sees that service and calls it great. Nothing is forgotten and in time he will promote you.

Martin Luther King, Jr realised this. He said, 'Everybody can be great … because anybody can serve. You don't have to have a college degree to serve. You don't have to make your subject and verb agree to serve. You only need a heart full of grace. A soul generated by love.'

I love what Shakespeare said about greatness. I'd just humbly add one thing: that all can choose greatness, because all can choose to serve. So go low and let God lift you up.

Grief

It's been said that grief is like an onion. I suppose because it makes your eyes water, and just when you think you're done you go and find another layer …

It is the human condition to enjoy the blessing of relationships. It is our burden to endure losing those we love. In the first Covid-19 lockdown, we lost my dear uncle, David. He fell down some stairs and hit his head. He never woke up from the coma. I've never been more grateful for having a dog collar. It was like a visa into an otherwise inaccessible country, allowing me to enter a hospital in lockdown, something that so many were tragically denied. I was able to go in three or four times and hold his hand, pray for him and finally commit him to God's keeping. It was one of the greatest honours of my life, but also one of the saddest. We loved him dearly. He was such fun to be with and always so gentle and generous. He was a judge in London and apparently once cycled off without having passed judgment at the end of a case! He quickly returned, thankfully. He loved Buddy Holly, so I played one of Buddy's songs as he lay there sleeping. I also played a hymn or two.

The poignancy of it all was almost overwhelming – seeing that my dear uncle really was but dust and that to dust he would soon return. But what caught me by surprise was how the grief began even before he died. I guess there comes a point with any very sick person when we know it's heading that way. I remember feeling it just after seeing my terminally ill friend, Adrian, in the summer of 2021. I just knew we'd hugged for the last time. I guess that's the way the deepest part of us prepares for what is coming. What a gift when we have time to say goodbye. Sadly, many aren't so lucky.

It's just so unyielding isn't it, death? So unforgiving. So harsh. So final. And the feelings that go with it – the shock, the sadness, the denial, the numbness, the anger, the questioning – the grief we experience, we sometimes wonder if we'll ever get through it. And sometimes, in some cases, we won't. I remember hearing a much-respected minister from a big central London church say that he believed a member of his congregation died from a broken heart following the loss of her husband. I think even the science would back that up. And why should that surprise us, when in marriage we become 'one flesh'?

You yourself may have experienced such a devastating and traumatic loss that it's simply unrealistic to expect significant change. I suppose all I'd want to speak into your heart and situation is, 'What is impossible with man is possible with God' (Luke 18:27). Yes, it may be a long journey. Yes, you might not get there fully in this life. But healing and comfort are available and you need not walk this path alone. I love the words of Psalm 23 that say, 'Yea, though I walk through the valley of the shadow of death, I will fear no evil; For You *are* with me; Your rod and Your staff, they comfort me' (*New King James Version* (*NKJV*), Psalm 23:4).

The inescapable truth is that we will all walk through that valley one day. Either accompanying someone we love or one

day passing that way ourselves. But God's promise to us is this: we need not fear, because he is with us. And just as surely as Jesus went into the grave but came back out, so this can be our story, too. What's more, we can know that God weeps with us in our pain. The shortest verse in the Bible comes when Jesus is at the tomb of his good friend Lazarus. It simply says, 'Jesus wept' (John 11:35). So we can take comfort; comfort that death is not the end, comfort that God is near us as we grieve, comfort that we're not alone.

Psalm 34 says, 'The Lord is close to the brokenhearted and saves those who are crushed in spirit' (Psalm 34:18). Is that you today? Are you struggling under a burden of grief and sadness that you just think will never end? Are you 'brokenhearted' or 'crushed in spirit'? If you are, then here's God's promise to you: he is close.

Now that might sound trite, or even unhelpful, given he's invisible, but I promise you, if you'd just reach out in faith, if you'd dare to believe he's there and call on him, he'll come to you and he'll bring hope and strength to your heart and comfort in your grief. You may not make it back to exactly where you were before – after all, we're never quite the same after losing someone we love – but you can know you're not alone and that in the crushing of grapes can come new wine.

Guidance

~

We live in a time when it's never been easier to get from A to B. Whether it's the Tube across town, a car journey across the country or a flight across the world, it's never been easier to find our way and choose our route. All you need is a smartphone and an app! And should you go wrong, which, let's face it, is often, well there's satnav to put us right.

Can anyone remember the day of paper maps in the car? It's a bygone era now and a bygone skill too it would seem! But I used to love having to work out the route and put one's plan to the test. Not that I'd take those days back, mind you. It's so gloriously easy now and such a time saver, and you can't stand in the way of progress (satnav will redirect you).

If only it was that simple in life. If only we had an 'on-board' guidance system for making the most important decisions in life. A voice in our ear or an app on our phone that could say, 'take the next right' or 'perform a U-turn imme-diately' (hopefully less of the latter). With any luck, we've all got people in our lives whose advice and voices we lean in to. People who know us well, love us deeply and want the best for our future. If you do, hold on to them tightly, because they're pure gold in a world of competing voices.

But is there more to find beyond that? A key that unlocks the secrets of life, the universe and what paths we should walk down? Humans have always believed there is, reaching for it through religion and philosophy. Many of my friends dabble with crystals, tarot cards and transcendental meditation. Others look to the stars (the heavenly kind, not Hollywood!), trusting their favourite astrologer to read their horoscope.

There's magic out there to be sure. And the wise men followed a star! But the thing I love most about the Christian story is how it points to a God who, far from staying at a distance, requiring you and me to grope about in the darkness trying to find him, came down, took on flesh, became human to come and find us. This is why Neil Armstrong, the first astronaut to do it, felt moved to say of Jesus Christ, 'It's a great thing for man to walk on the moon. But it's a greater thing for God to walk on the Earth.' Jesus is truly the 'Good Shepherd' who longs to come alongside his sheep and even find them when they go astray. Is there a more gracious sovereign out there?

So let me ask you, do you feel lost at this strange time? Or if not lost, then a bit errant or all at sea? Because shepherding is possible with this shepherd and guidance is possible with this guide.

For Christians, there are many ways in which we believe God speaks to us and guides us. There's the Bible for one thing! In it we believe God has made his thoughts and opinions known and that he's still speaking those words today. This means that the words come to us, still hot with the breath of God. I've experienced God guiding me through his word many, many times. Once, when I was exploring the idea of ordination (getting a dog collar) in the Church of England, I went to an open day at Wycliffe Hall theology college in Oxford. The opening reflection was drawn from John's Gospel, chapter 21, when Jesus asks Peter if he loves him, and then commands him to 'feed my sheep'. Strong passage, I thought. We then had a brief service in their chapel, where the speaker began by apologising for the fact that, entirely by chance, he would be preaching from exactly the same scripture. Interesting, I thought. Having returned to London that evening, I decided to go to church (it was a Sunday). You can imagine the goosebumps I felt when Revd Sandy Millar stood up and spoke from the very same verses. OK Lord, I thought, you've got my attention now.

Christians also believe that God is active in the world through the third person of the Trinity, the Holy Spirit. He's as equally God as the Father and the Son, and he's the one who connects us to God in the here and now. He also leads and guides his people and could use anything under heaven, or within heaven for that matter. Be it a lyric in a song, a quote from a film, a bill-board, a conversation or an angel – he can literally use anything. Or he might bring thoughts or pictures to mind or even guide our very steps. I remember a lady sharing how the Holy Spirit revealed to her a street name and house number that turned out to be in the town where she was looking for a home. The house was for sale and she now lives there!

Then there are other ways in which God might guide us, like through the wisdom and counsel of friends. We all know that it's good to chat things through with those who love and know us best. Common sense is also a gift from God to help steer us, although it's true that some seem to have more of it than others ...

Finally, because we believe that 'The earth is the Lord's, and everything in it, the world, and all who live in it' (Psalm 24:1), we believe that every single moment can be one where God is speaking because God can use any part of his creation. Some may call these moments 'coincidences', but when you believe in God you know there's no such thing. So Christians call them 'circumstantial signs', and it can be pretty fun when they happen. One agnostic friend of mine was wrestling with the bigger questions of life and whether there might be more, when he happened to bump into me three times in as many weeks in a supermarket in Parsons Green. He took it as a sign that he should come to church and then proceeded to do Alpha, a course that explores the Christian faith. It really helped him.

Now I'm not saying that if you become a Christian, you'll know exactly what to do and never put a foot wrong. Goodness knows I've made mistakes! But the invitation to us all is to know the one who knows all things and who can lovingly lead and guide us.

For me, since having faith, it feels more like going through life with the headlights on than driving in the dark. Not that I always know where I'm going or can see super clearly or far ahead. But you have enough light for the next step and, when you've got that, you can confidently take it, with hope in your heart.

Healing

Life hurts. From our earliest memories, we know this – that grazed knee, that bruised arm, that unkind word, that painful loss. But just as we quickly learn that many of these things get better with time, we have to believe that better days are ahead. Because it's hard to have hope when we don't think things can change, when we don't think that healing is possible.

You may be carrying around wounds from the past, scars and memories that just don't seem to let you go. You struggle to find freedom. You find it hard to move on. Add to that the age of social media, when everyone else seems to be 'living their best life', with no worries at all, and the sense of failure and despondency just increases.

And yet we sense there must be more. We see goodness everywhere – light amid the darkness … receiving the kindness of a stranger, someone handing in your lost wallet on the bus, a family being reunited. Dare we believe that healing is possible?

I believe we can. In the gospels, we see something remarkable. Jesus came, speaking about a different kingdom to the one we see and touch. He was referring to the kingdom of God, a realm of light and love and fulfilment, where there's room for all and everyone's invited. He said turn around (repent) and believe the good news. And then he demonstrated that kingdom – he healed the sick, he raised the dead, he broke down strongholds and he welcomed outcasts. That's why the people flocked to him. Something supernatural was taking place.

Now, at the outset I want to be honest. In my walk with God, I've seen far fewer healings than I would like. And that can be tough to accept. We're often left confused or disappointed when our prayers aren't answered how we would like them to be – when our situation doesn't change or a loved one or friend doesn't get better. But the absence of a miracle isn't reason not to ask. Nor is it evidence that God doesn't care or is not listening. So we'll keep on praying, and not give up.

Because it's still happening today. Down the ages, people can testify to the healing power of God in their lives. Not just physically, but emotionally and spiritually too. I've known and experienced it in my own life. And because God is outside time, he can go back to that painful moment, to that word or action or trauma, and knit us back together, leaving a perfectly healed wound. Yes, we might bear the scar, but it will no longer bring us pain.

I experienced this powerfully when I was 22. For many years, I'd been aware of a deep angst and insecurity. I'd be doing fine, but then at any given moment this anxiety would just rise up within me, quickening my heart rate and disturbing my peace. It was a very unsettling feeling. I'd experienced it from about the age of 10 but had put it down to 'growing pains'. One day, however, when I was in a time of worship and prayer, it began to rise up strongly. This time, I'd just had enough. So I went after it with God. I prayed something like, 'Lord, I've had enough of this thing. I want to be free of it. What the heck is it and where does it come from, because I don't believe you want me to have it!' And, quick as a flash, in my mind's eye (I had my eyes shut, praying), I saw a scene from my childhood. It was when my brother and I were in the sitting room of a new house we'd recently moved into, as we'd lost our old one following the defrauding of my father's business. We were watching TV when Mum came into the room, turned off the telly and, as gently as she could, told us that she and Dad were splitting up. My whole world was rocked. Panic hit me. And what the Lord showed me in this vision was that, in that moment, trauma entered my heart. And I'd been living with it ever since.

That's what would manifest at any given moment; that's what would suddenly rise up in me. And, as God showed me this, I just wept. I wept with the pain and memory of it all. I wept as I remembered what was lost. But the amazing thing is that those tears soon turned to joy as I experienced God's touch and healing in my heart. It was literally as if God had taken me back to an open wound that had never properly healed, and had sewn me up again, binding me back together. Because, from that moment, I stopped experiencing the angst and unease that had flowed from that untreated trauma. The great physician had come and healed me, and he can heal where you hurt, too.

In fact, he did that just a few days ago for a lady in our church. We'd been in a month of prayer and held an evening of prayer on Friday from 6pm until midnight. Beatriz came along and then messaged me that night. She's given me permission to share her story:

Hi Pat,
I just wanted to say thank you to the church family for organising today. Ever since I became a mother 22 months ago, I

felt like time was not on my side. I've been so caught up with motherhood that at times I have forgotten about God.

When I got to church this evening, I was praying to God to touch me, to show me a sign or a vision. Nothing happened. When you asked if anyone wanted a prayer, I put my hand up and Maggie, Belinda and another lady prayed for me. I've been suffering from a bad back ever since I was pregnant. Maggie was praying for me and, all of a sudden, I felt like I was being pushed, I was unsteady on my feet and it was as if something was leaving my body and I felt this wave of electricity all over my body. I've never ever felt anything like this in my Christian life.

I'd come to believe that God only speaks to certain people, but tonight I got proven wrong. I feel so light, like the world has been lifted off my shoulders.

Are you hurting today? Does your hope feel crushed? Are you in need of healing? You can call on God right now, because one of his names is Jehovah-Rapha, which means, 'The Lord Who Heals'.

Identity

We all just want to know who we are, don't we? From the beginning of time, human beings have told stories, established values and created frameworks that have sought to shape and define themselves. Some have been healthy, others destructive, but all have recognised that there is an inherent desire in each of us to know where we come from, know where we're going and know life to the full in between.

Rarely have we seen the question of identity so contested or confused as it appears to be right now. And that's no great surprise. In a globalised age, where every culture and creed is connected, there's never been such a plethora of outlooks and world views to choose from. I struggle to choose which coffee to buy, let alone which tradition or 'truth' to live in. It can all seem too much! The American singer–songwriter Taylor Swift captured this experience perfectly in her NYU commencement speech in 2022 when she said, 'We are so many things, all the time. And I know it can be overwhelming figuring out who to be ... I have some good news: It's totally up to you. I also have some terrifying news: it's totally up to you.'

Indeed that would be terrifying! But what if it wasn't 'totally' up to us? What if, just as there are physical laws that govern what's possible, there were spiritual laws as well? What if there really is a creator, who knows why and how he made us and wants to communicate that to us? Wouldn't we want that conversation? Wouldn't we seek out that perspective? Because the chaos we feel within ourselves, and then see played out in the world, comes when we make 'us' the starting point; when we make it all about you and me. It's hard not to do that, because everywhere we go, there we are! But what if we don't have all the data? What if our frame of reference isn't enough?

What if we could just ask our creator, the designer and lover of our souls? All I can say is that my faith has helped bring light into darkness, clarity to confusion and simple truth where I needed it most. I believe it can help you, too.

When God appears to Moses in a burning bush, he says that his name is 'I AM WHO I AM' (Exodus 3:14). I always find that amazing – that God Almighty has a name! And names are very important. They tell the world and ourselves who we are. So let me ask you, what's your name? I don't primarily mean what people call you – like 'Pat' – but perhaps more how people see you or even how you see yourself. Perhaps it's 'the funny one' or 'the kind one' or 'the dependable one'. Or perhaps there are more negative names that the world has given you or that you've even given yourself, such as 'the hopeless one', 'the unlucky one', 'the unhappy one' or 'the unreliable one'.

It can be a battle to have clarity on our identity, which is why faith is such a gift. Because just as God has a name, he can give us ours too. In a world where so many other things, people or pressures are trying to shape us, mould us, define us, ultimately, God alone knows who we are, how he made us, where we come from and where we're going.

Because he's been there all along. He was there right from the start: 'In the beginning was the Word, and the Word was with God, and the Word was God' (John 1:1). Christians believe that Jesus is that Word and that he has shaped all things.

And the incredible thing is that even he knows how hard it is to feel truly understood and accepted in this world. After all, look at what happened to him! But here's the simple truth: you are known and you are loved. And you're invited to come as you are. Just don't expect to stay that way. God's plans for us are just too big for us to come to on our own terms. The future's holy and it is glorious and we must prepare for it. But if we draw near with childlike faith, if we call out humbly, admitting our flaws and limitations, then we'll find what we are looking for – a rock to stand on and eyes to see. And, more importantly, we'll find out who we are.

Joy

There's nothing better than laughing right? Everything seems OK when we're doing that. After all, it's hard to be laughing but also miserable at the same time. It's a gift, a release, even healthy. But it's also our highest good and end. But I'm not talking about cheap thrills or crude jokes. I'm not even talking about happiness, because there's a difference between happiness and joy.

Happiness is circumstantial. Happiness is event-driven. It's outcome-dependent, which means that, if things don't go our way, our happy state can very quickly turn sour. We're smiling when the sun is shining, then the rain clouds come. We're buzzing when that special person is texting, then they find someone new. We're happy at work with all the good things it brings, then we get laid off. And ultimately, life is good when our nearest and dearest are all safe and well, but then one hits hard times, another gets sick and someone we love very much just dies. How does happiness cope with that?

The truth is, it doesn't. Because it was never made to. It simply doesn't have the resources to endure. It's too based in circumstance, which is why we need joy. Pure, unadulterated joy; the good stuff … Joy that's not dependent on whether your team won or lost that weekend. Joy that's not shaken when that certain someone fails to text you back (crushing though that is). Joy that endures no matter what life throws at us. Joy that laughs in the face of sorrow. But how and where do we find such joy?

There's a verse in the Bible that says, 'the joy of the Lord is your strength' (Nehemiah 8:10). For me, this has always been a huge encouragement because it promises that, whatever I face in life, however big the challenges and my need to persevere, I have the strength and resources to do it. Not because of something I've done or possess in and of myself, but because of God's joy that lives within me. I guess this can either be understood as joy that flows from knowing the giver of life or the joy he has within himself. Either way, a lot of joy is on offer!

And that joy can never be taken from you, because no one can ever take it from him, and he's the one who gives it to us. So circumstances are no longer King. Our happiness doesn't depend on the weather anymore. Our joy can be solid, reliable and unchanging, because it rests in the joy-giver. And he is joyful. Oh my goodness, God is the happiest being in the universe! Outside of it too … He's delighted with himself (in the right way) and has a great time every day.

Doesn't that sound like fun? I don't know about you, but I'm so bored of the world's empty promises. I'm fed up with the fragility of what it offers. Whether it's the hollow claims of politicians or that materialism can truly satisfy us. If my ultimate joy and happiness depend on anyone else, or even on myself, then we might as well give up, because we will always be let down. And we'll live in constant anxiety and uncertainty.

But if it's dependent on God, who is 'the same yesterday and today and forever' (Hebrews 13:8), and we trust in him, then we can rest and relax in that knowledge, knowing that good things are coming in this life and, worst-case scenario, if we meet our demise prematurely, good things are coming in the next.

Ask yourself this: where is your life source flowing from? Where do you look for true happiness and fulfilment? And then ask yourself, how secure is that thing? Will it outlast the storms of life and even endure into eternity?

During the Covid-19 pandemic, I posted an Instagram story with these words: 'If your world view doesn't equip you to deal with end-of-the-world scenarios, it's time you got an upgrade.' Faith in God is that upgrade. We need a joy that's untouchable by life! Because, without it, how can we truly have hope? Too much depends on the winds of chance and it could all go horribly wrong in a moment.

Only God lives forever; he and those to whom he gives eternal life. I don't know about you, but I want that life. I want that joy. And here's the thing, once you have confidence about the big things – knowing where you've come from and where you're going – you can relax and enjoy the ride. You can kick back and take things as they come. Because even if you may have unhappy times, you need never be without joy deep down.

Joy is like the ocean's deep; happiness is like the ocean's surface. There might be waves up top, making you nervous as heck, but deep down you can know peace and joy, as that's a depth nothing in this life can touch.

Justice

As I write this, I honestly feel overwhelmed by the scale and nature of some of the topics we're looking at. They're just huge! And so nuanced and multifaceted. And here's another one: justice.

I think we all have an inherent sense of right and wrong, what's fair and what's unfair. Just look at children: 'They got more than me ...'/'They didn't close their eyes when I hid!' Where does this sense come from? Well, one foundational element of the Judeo-Christian tradition is that we're all made in God's image, made with dignity and worth. It's important to stress the influence that this simple truth has had on the world, giving us principles for ethics as well as a framework for structuring society and continually re-forming it.

All of this goes into shaping our understanding of justice – the basic idea that people should be treated with dignity and respect and that there should be consequences for those who fall short. But it's hard to have an agreed-upon concept of justice if we don't have some broadly agreed-upon concept of 'the good'. For Christians, this objective standard is underpinned and guaranteed by the reality of God and his Word. And in it, boy do we find a high bar for justice. For taking care of the poor and the needy. For providing for the widowed and the orphaned.

Indeed, Psalm 89 tells us that 'righteousness and justice are the foundation of your throne' (Psalm 89:14). I'd go as far as to say that justice is only possible because there's justice at the heart of creation, at the heart of the creator. It's not just chaos. It's not all meaningless. We're not here by chance.

Inherent to the Christian tradition is the idea of a God who has opinions on what's right and wrong, and who lovingly made the world and set humanity in it as his 'image bearers', to rule and steward it on his behalf. And just as he promises to do justice at the end of time, he calls us all to pursue it here and now.

The idea of God bringing ultimate justice to this world may make us nervous. After all, haven't we had a hand in contributing to its many injustices? Be it through fast fashion, cheap flights and climate change, or simply not doing the good that we should, we all fall short, don't we? And just as we cry out for justice for the seemingly big things, should we not face it too for the small things we've done? Hmm, suddenly it feels slightly less appealing …

Injustice takes many forms. And it varies in degree. But it all stems from one place – within the human heart. You see, it isn't what goes into someone that's the issue. It isn't external circumstance or conditioning, influential though those are, that ultimately lead to an unjust world. Rather, it's what comes out of us that's the problem. As Jesus says, 'For out of the heart come evil thoughts – murder, adultery, sexual immorality, theft, false testimony, slander. These are what defile a person' (Matthew 15:19–20).

The Russian author and dissident Aleksandr Solzhenitsyn captured this idea when he wrote, 'The line separating good and evil passes not through states, nor between classes, nor between political parties either – but right through every human heart – and through all human hearts.'

And isn't that true, when we're really honest with ourselves? We know how we'd like to live and speak and react and treat other people. We even know the kind of fashion we should buy and the kind of travel we should avoid. And yet we keep on making the same decisions. We can't seem to help ourselves. Why? Because it comes from inside of us. It comes from the human heart. What does this have to do with justice, you might ask? Well, before we can hope to bring justice to our world, we must first face justice inside ourselves.

A scary thought, you might well think. And it is, but there's good news. Because precisely where we are guilty of falling short of the virtues we all agree with and may even occasionally like to signal, thus contributing to injustice in our world, Jesus comes and takes our place. He literally takes the blame for us, like a scapegoat or sacrificial lamb. It's hard to get your head around, and there's real mystery to it, but somehow, on the cross, Jesus took responsibility for everything you and I have ever done wrong. He carried all our unjust acts and received the judgment we deserve. And in return, if we come to him, well the blessings are too great to number, but they include forgiveness, a fresh start, relationship with God, eternal life, hope, joy and peace.

Does this mean we are freed from responsibility and can go on living as we please? Not at all! Rather, we must continue and redouble our efforts to work and strive towards a more just and fair society. Far from letting us off the hook, the example of Jesus should bring us fresh vision and motivation to seek the good of others in everything we do. The way of Jesus is the way of love. And as has been said, 'Justice is what love looks like in public.' So let's go public with our love!

Of course, you don't need faith to have a heart for justice, but I think it strengthens it. Because when you believe the big picture – that there's one God and creator of us all – when you realise that every person is made in his image, precious and dearly loved by him, including you, then that begins to shape your thinking and you catch a different vision for your life, one where justice is absolutely key.

As such, Christians have often been at the forefront of the fight for justice in society and social transformation in our world. Be it the campaign to abolish the slave trade, led so enduringly by William Wilberforce, the reforms to working conditions in factories and mines and opposing the practice of child labour, as pursued by Lord Shaftesbury, or the more recent civil rights movement in America, spearheaded by the inspirational Martin Luther King, Jr.

Another name you may be familiar with is Rosa Parks, whose brave and defiant act of disobedience, in the face of shameless and endemic racism, helped spark the civil rights movement. On the evening of 1 December 1955, Rosa took the bus home and sat in an empty seat at the front of the section reserved for Black people. As the bus began to fill up however, the driver moved the sign saying 'colored' behind Rosa and three other people and told them to give up their seats. The other three did, but Rosa remained seated. When asked why she didn't get up, she replied, 'I don't think I should have to stand up.' When the driver then said that if she didn't stand up, he'd have to call the police and she would be arrested, Rosa later wrote that, 'I instantly felt God give me the strength to endure whatever would happen next. God's peace flooded my soul, and my fear

melted away.' And so she calmly replied, 'You may do that.'

She was arrested, convicted and fined. But she didn't give up. She went on to appeal against her conviction, challenging the very legality of racial segregation. Her case, backed by civil rights groups, churches and others, went all the way to the Supreme Court, where segregation was ruled unconstitutional. Truly a modern David and Goliath story! The great evil of racism, slain by a humble, faith-filled 42-year-old woman.

We might not all be Martin Luther King, Jrs, but we can all take our stand (or stay seated!) like Rosa. If the Christian story is true, it means there's fairness at the heart of the universe. It means that justice is worth pursuing and that it will one day come in full.

Kindness

~

I love Charlie Mackesy's book, *The Boy, the Mole, the Fox and the Horse*. It's full of positive and hopeful thoughts. One of his pictures has these words, "'Nothing beats kindness,' said the horse. "It sits quietly beyond all things".'

If I asked you to bring to mind the teacher who's had the biggest impact on your life, I'd wager there'd be a shared quality to all our choices ... kindness. It's often the kindness of people we remember. Their warmth and generosity of spirit. It's wonderful to be on the receiving end, but it's just as special to give it!

My brother, Will, is very kind. He's not a Christian, but is naturally kind and generous. I often say that it took supernatural help to make me kind, and I'm still a work in progress! It took me finding God to bring about that fruit, whilst he just seemed to have it! I remember one time when we were kids, I was 10 and he was 12, and we were on Exmoor having a family picnic. It was a hot day, so we were topless and only wearing shorts. My brother really annoyed me for some reason (I'd probably requested something very unreasonable to which he'd said no) and so, in my anger, I pushed him backwards into a gorse bush, fully knowing that it was there. I don't know if you're familiar with gorse, but it's the kind of stuff that if your arm just brushes it, you go 'ow'. And there he was, fully immersed in the stuff! Well, he somehow flew out of that bush and came straight after me. I've never run so fast in my life, but it wasn't fast enough, and he hauled me to the ground. Pinning me down, he had every right to belt me or shove sheep dung in my mouth, but as I cried out for mercy, the last thing I deserved, his face softened and he let me go. In fact, come to think of it, I can't ever remember my brother hurting me growing up. He was always protective, always kind. Goodness me, he showed me the face of God. Indeed, my dad's always said that if I'd had any other older brother, I wouldn't have lived past the age of five!

If there's one thing our world needs, it's kindness. It just feels like there's all too little, right? Be it online, in schools or in politics. It just feels as though, as life gets busier, people are getting more and more frayed at the edges. When we then turn and bump into others, we don't always overflow with the milk of human kindness. They don't get the best version of us. In fact, sometimes, they get quite the opposite!

Maybe it's helpful to think of ourselves as having a kindness tank. The fuller it is, the more we can give. So how do we fill our tank? Well, spiritually, as with many things that we've seen, the more we understand what we've received, the more freely we will give. And in Jesus, God has shown us unending kindness. He hasn't treated us as we deserve but sent his Son to find and bring us home. He's always patient, always compassionate, always gentle, always kind.

There's a time very near the end of Jesus' life when he gathers his disciples together for what's called 'the last supper'. It's when he washes their feet, does some final teaching and institutes the Eucharist with bread and wine. But one of the things that amazes me most about that last meal is how Jesus continues to extend the hand of kindness to Judas, even though he knows he's about to betray him. We know this, because Jesus is sitting close enough to give him a piece of bread. Now, I'm well aware of the expression (and the wisdom of it!) 'keep your friends close and your enemies closer', but this was something different. Because Jesus wasn't afraid of what was coming, his betrayal and crucifixion. No, he never shrank from his primary calling, the very reason why he came. Instead, I think he was more concerned about Judas' soul, and was seeking to reach out in love and kindness, believing and hoping for the best, right till the very end.

Because that's the nature of kindness – it doesn't distinguish between good or bad, friend or foe. True kindness is always there, extending the generous hand of friendship, to anyone and everyone. Loving its enemies, blessing those who curse it, praying for those who persecute it. And Jesus models this because that's what God is like. 'He causes his sun to rise on the evil and the good, and sends rain on the righteous and the unrighteous' (Matthew 5:45).

I don't always get this right by any means, and too often I'm impatient or get frustrated. But occasionally an opportunity presents itself and I feel I've done the right thing. There was a time when I lived in London in a sort of gated community. You needed a fob to get in or out. My beloved old bike was coming to the end of its life and I think I'd lost the lock or something, because I'd decided just to leave it unlocked outside in the bike zone. Truth be told, I was wondering how to get rid of it. But, one day, driving back in through the gates, I saw a chap waiting on the other side to get out, with none other than my mountain bike. Now, I know I was wondering how to get rid of it, but I didn't have this in mind. I hopped out of my car and gently challenged him about what he was doing. He said he was leaving with his bike. When I politely informed him that it was actually my bike, he backed down and went very quiet. It was then that compassion surprised me. So, as unpatronisingly as I could, I asked why he was doing this, and encouraged him not to go down this path as it wouldn't end well for him. I tried to call out a better future, saying there was a God in heaven who loved him and who had good plans for him, if he'd look to him and pursue a different path. He seemed surprisingly open to listening. Or perhaps he was just glad I wasn't phoning the police! But I tell you what, it brought me alive to act like this, to choose kindness instead of harshness, mercy instead of judgement. On reflection, I'm only sorry I didn't gift him the bike. But we're all works in progress ... perhaps next time.

I think these opportunities are there for each one of us every single day – be it turning the other cheek, going the extra mile, bringing a kind word instead of a harsh one, speaking well of someone behind their back rather than joining in the gossip, fetching that colleague a glass of water, helping that commuter with their bags. When you actually stop to think about it, there's no end to what we could do. Even more so when we become part of communities that seek to live this way. On a similar front, when our Worship Pastor Joe moved down to London from Nottingham, his bike was stolen within 48 hours of arriving (I really hope it wasn't my guy). So we put the word out on our church WhatsApp group and within a few days we'd raised more than £700 for him to buy a new one.

We all want to change the world. We all hope for a better future. But we usually think it requires great deeds, international agreement, the right laws and policies. But what if we just started where we were and let the little things add up? If we did what we could, where we could and formed communities that did the same? As has been said, 'Never doubt that a small group of thoughtful committed individuals can change the world. In fact, it's the only thing that ever has.'

This is the way of Jesus. Transforming individuals and transforming communities. So, in an often unkind world, turn to him to fill your tank. Then give kindness freely away, because you can always come back for more, there's a never-ending supply …

Loneliness

'There are many in the world who are dying for a piece of bread but there are many more dying for a little love. The poverty in the West is a different kind of poverty – it is ... a poverty of loneliness.' So said Mother Teresa. And who better to understand this reality than one who devoted her life to the poorest of the poor.

The great challenge of our time is loneliness. We live in a world that is more connected than ever before. At the touch of a button or a screen, we can be communicating with people on the other side of the world. People we haven't even met! And yet, despite this relational revolution, we are lonelier than ever before. We've all known those moments, I'm sure. Where we know on paper we've got so much, we know from our contacts list we've got lots of friends, we know from our diary we've got things going on, but, deep down, we just feel lonely.

I write this entry on the back of two years of enforced lockdowns and isolation as a result of the Covid-19 pandemic. This was devastating on many fronts, not least of which was an increased sense of loneliness. We all experienced that – what an extraordinary moment of shared human consciousness. In many ways, this was understandable – we were cut off from one another, denied seeing or visiting one another, unable to visit the places we love, with people we love, doing things that we love. It was lonely!

But what about the times when we're not in lockdown, when there's no global pandemic, no mandatory isolation required and we do what on earth we like? What's the solution when we still feel lonely then?

Freddie Mercury, the late lead singer of the rock band Queen, captured this when he said in the *Rock on, Freddie* interview:

> You can have everything in the world and still be the loneliest man. And that is the most bitter type of loneliness. Success has brought me world idolisation and millions of pounds. But it's prevented me from having the one thing we all need: a loving, ongoing relationship.

And I suppose that's why, for me, faith has been such a game-changer when it comes to loneliness.

I love a party as much as the next person. I love gatherings, people and fun. But none of that, and no other human, can ultimately meet our needs. Because nothing and no one else can ever be with us all the time. Maybe that's why we're so addicted to our phones, a friend who will 'never leave'!

In Matthew's Gospel, God's name is revealed as 'Immanuel', meaning 'God with us' (Matthew 1:23). I love this. It means that when we receive him, we'll never be alone again: wherever we go, he's there with us; whatever we do, he's by our side. And not just that, we can talk with him and he with us. We can know his presence at all times. What greater comfort is there than that? What other companion do we need?

In one of my favourite scriptures, God promises, 'Never will

I leave you; never will I forsake you' (Hebrews 13:5). Wow, what a promise. Friends may leave you, spouses may leave you, even your own mother or father may leave you. But God will never leave you. He wants to be 'best friends forever'. He wants you in his family.

As the inspirational Archbishop Desmond Tutu said, 'The solitary human being is a contradiction in terms ... We are made for complementarity. We are created for a delicate network of relationships, of interdependence with our fellow human beings ... We belong in one family – God's family.'

And it's not just the blessing of knowing God and getting to be in relationship with him, the vertical axis if you like. No, he also designed us to be in families and, ultimately, part of his family, the Church – the horizontal axis as it were. There's a beautiful verse that says, 'God sets the lonely in families' (Psalm 68:6). That was my experience when I became a Christian. I suddenly found that I had lots more brothers and sisters, and spiritual mothers and fathers. Not that they replace our blood family – they don't, and we wouldn't want them to – but you find a community and depth of relationship that's just not possible anywhere else, or at least it hadn't been for me. God's heart and plan is to bring the whole world together in Christ. To make one family of every nation. We'll only see this fully in the age to come, but we can aim for it today.

We'll all experience loneliness – it's just part of the human journey – but there's one who'll walk alongside us if we'd just reach out and take his hand. And, when we do, we find him, but we also find each other and so much more.

Love

~

What else? Apparently, it's all we need ...! And do you know what? The Beatles absolutely nailed it, theologically as well as in every other way, when they wrote that line.

From the beginning of time, human beings have been inspired by, moved by, consumed by love. It's been the foundation of society and the muse for artists and authors through the ages. As Ewan McGregor says to Nicole Kidman in one of my favourite films, *Moulin Rouge!*, 'Love is a many-splendoured thing. Love lifts us up where we belong.'

But why is this the case, and how can we capture its essence and say anything meaningful about it? Well, the Ancient Greeks gave it a good try. Indeed they had seven different words for love: 'philia', which speaks of friendship; 'ludus', which describes playful, flirtatious love; 'storge', which is unconditional, familial love; 'philautia', which is compassionate self-love (which we're pretty good at these days!); 'eros', which describes passionate, romantic love; 'pragma', which concerns commitment and long-standing love; and, finally, 'agape', which captures empathetic, universal love for everyone.

Those Greeks were wise, hey? And they, along with every other human being and culture that has developed under the sun, were on to something, because they were discerning and tapping into the underlying fabric and DNA of the universe. Because the Bible says that 'God is love' (1 John 4:8) and, if everything we have and are comes from God, then truly, all we need is love.

But how do we know that life should be all about love? I mean, if there's no purpose or meaning to the universe, then survival should be our priority, right? But that would make us rivals and competitors, not the best seedbed for fostering self-sacrificial love. And yet we see that all around us, and our art and film and music are full of it, honouring and celebrating it.

You see, at the end of the day, life is all about stories. And we have to live in one, as we've seen. When it comes to love or hatred, light or darkness, hope or despair, there's enough evidence on either side for you to choose your narrative accordingly. Which path will you go down? Which story will you live in? Because ahead of all else, that will determine your hope and your joy, your treatment of others and yourself.

That's why I think we all know it. That's why the Beatles wrote songs all about it. Because the song of heaven goes out into all creation, speaking of the one who made it, who loves it and who came to redeem it in his Son. And we were made to join in and sing ...

One of the most famous verses in the Bible is, 'For God so loved the world that he gave his one and only Son, that whoever believes in him shall not perish but have eternal life' (John 3:16). So, if nothing else, always know that God's first and greatest feeling towards you is love. It underpins everything he is and everything he does.

And this loving God loves you and me. But life gets really

interesting when you come to experience his love for yourself! That's literally what's on offer through Christ. For me, that's what changed everything. When I prayed a prayer to the ceiling, inviting God into my life, he came in. He filled me with his Holy Spirit, which simply felt like liquid love, joy, peace and hope, filling me up on the inside. That's nice, you might think; but here's the thing, it's not just for our benefit and enjoyment, as wonderful as it is. No, it's all to be given away! My encounter with God, finding the one who can fill me up, has made me more loving to those around me. Not just that, but more joyful, peaceful, patient, kind, good (better!), faithful, gentle and self-controlled. All the fruit of the Holy Spirit! It's made me more of the person that, deep down, I always wanted to be.

On the inside of our wedding rings, my wife Kirsty and I both have engraved the words, 'Love always …' Now, that's not just a sentiment about timeline aspirations, but is also a quote from perhaps the most popularly read scripture at weddings, 1 Corinthians 13. It's a scripture that simply but beautifully outlines what love looks like. I encourage you to give it a read:

> Love is patient, love is kind. It does not envy, it does not boast, it is not proud. It does not dishonor others, it is not self-seeking, it is not easily angered, it keeps no record of wrongs. Love does not delight in evil but rejoices with the truth. It always protects, always trusts, always hopes, always perseveres.

I remember hearing someone say how, in order to take a self-inventory of sorts to see how they're doing on the whole love front, they simply sub in their name where it says 'love', and then ask themselves if it's true. Where it's not, there's work to do – a truly revealing, if humbling/terrifying exercise.

There's a line that preachers love to say about Jesus hanging on the cross, which is something like, 'It wasn't the nails that held him there, but his love for you and me.'

As Jesus hung there on that cross, about to breathe his last, he didn't have revenge in mind, thinking of those who'd done him harm. He didn't have regret in mind, wondering if he could have done things a different way. He had us in mind. It was always all about us, and our loved ones, and their loved ones too … Meaning everyone's invited, there's enough love to go around!

Love is truly all we need, and in faith we can receive it.

Marriage

At the time of writing this, I am exactly 10 months and 9 days married, which, you may say, might not position me ideally to pontificate much about marriage. And you'd be right. Add to that the fact that my parents divorced when I was 10 and your case is even stronger! However, as I occasionally point out when I speak at weddings, my mother and stepfather are on their fifth marriage between them (maybe sixth, it's their third each!), so that's got to be worth something ... even if just as an objective observer.

Marriage is a blessing. I love my wife immensely. But goodness, marriage is also hard. Especially when you come to it late, like I did. And I don't so much mean the toothpaste thing or how cold or hot you like the bedroom (cold is always better). No, I mean learning to think about, plan for and take care of another person. As my good friend John once said (whom I'm sure got it from somewhere), 'marriage is the school of unselfishness'. He went on to add, 'and having kids is the PhD'! And it's just so true. But what a blessing that it's true. Because, boy, do I need to go to school. I could probably do with a nursery or Montessori first, to be fair ...

But it's hard isn't it? Why didn't anyone tell me? I'm (semi) joking, but of course it is, because when you marry someone, you fundamentally change. In fact, the Bible says that you become so close, so intertwined, that you become 'one flesh' (Genesis 2:24).

And marriage is a joy, a wonder, a blessing in creation. A place of mutual support, encouragement and flourishing. A 'holy estate', as the Book of Common Prayer puts it. A place for, God willing, having children and nurturing them.

But did I mention it's challenging too? My wife is the easiest-going person, so, just to be clear, it's me who has all the issues. But our marriage aside, it's clear that it's a challenge. The UK divorce rate is estimated to be around 42 per cent. That's higher than I scored in my Land Law exam the first time round, and about what I got when I retook it. It's not good. But it perhaps helps explain a joke I always tell at all the weddings that I take (very much tongue-in-cheek):

I've heard marriage described like a game of cards.
At the start, all you need are two hearts and a diamond.
In the end, all you want are a club and a spade.

The trouble is, many people go into marriage with the wrong expectations. They think its primary purpose is to make them happy. Now, please don't mishear me, I'm not for a moment saying it doesn't or that you should expect to be miserable for the rest of your days. Happiness is a core hope, goal and fruit of marriage! But when choppy waters inevitably come (or even arrive on honeymoon), when it feels more like wading through the waves than surfing on them, so to speak, it's then that it's worth remembering the real purpose of marriage. And according to the Christian tradition, it's less to make us happy and more to make us holy. We're back in unselfish school again, as well as sifting out every other kind of vice and instilling virtues in their place.

You see, holiness – in other words, looking like God, who is pure light – is the goal of any marriage. It's the goal of any life actually, whether married or single!

There's a beautiful blessing that sometimes gets used at weddings that brings this out:

> The God of heaven so join you now that you may be glad of one another all your lives. And when he that has joined you shall separate you, may he again establish you with an assurance that he has but borrowed one of you for a time to make both more perfect in the resurrection.

God's goal is our perfection. And, just like gold, we need refining. So if it's hard just now, hold on, because more value is being added ... and marriage is worth fighting for! Because out of marriage comes family and, as Pope John Paul II said, 'As the family goes, so goes the nation and so goes the whole world in which we live.'

Having said all that, it's also important to stress that marriage is not the be-all and end-all by any means – you're not incomplete if you don't have it. Jesus himself was single and he's the most fulfilled person who's ever lived! That said, it can be very hard and painful if it's what you want but it just hasn't happened. But it's worth keeping in mind that in heaven, no one's married, so you could say single people are ahead of the game! That's not to say loved ones aren't reunited in heaven, simply that there'll be a different order of relationships.

But the most breathtaking news is this: God wants to marry

you and me. Meaning he wants unending, joy-filled, intimate relationship. He wants to be with us forever. That's where the whole thing points! And everyone's included and invited. As incredible as it sounds, the Church is the 'bride' of Christ, which means that one day he's coming back to get her. And then, there's going to be a wedding and a party that goes on forever, where the music never stops and the wine never runs out …

So if you want 'in', if you're keen to be 'married' to God, then just choose faith and say yes to his proposal in Christ.

Meaning

Do we know what we're living for?

The prevailing world view of the West, really since the Enlightenment, has been that of secular humanism, which claims that there is no God and we're all here by chance. The BBC presenter, physicist, author and ex-synth player for the band D:Ream, Professor Brian Cox, whose work I greatly admire, articulated this tribe's perspective on meaning when he said in the podcast *The Infinite Monkey Cage*:

> Every human, therefore, is a thing of great significance in a restricted but important sense. On a cosmic scale, our physical presence is of no consequence. We are temporary assemblies of ten billion billion billion atoms, and in a century or less, they will all be returned for recycling. But for the briefest of moments these atoms are able to contemplate themselves. They will spend an eternity in darkness when we are gone. Our purpose should be to extend their moment in the light as best we can.

I 100 per cent agree. If there is no God, that is …

But if there is, then everything has changed and the offer of spending eternity in the light is very real!

Many would say that we only pursue this question of meaning because we're scared to face reality; that we somehow need there to be meaning in order to avoid chaos and despair. After all, if there isn't a creator with a plan or design, then we really are just here by chance, a fluke of nature, on a rock, spinning round a star. And if that's the case, then other than our mutually agreed standards and laws, what's to stop us tearing each other apart and bringing the whole house crashing down? You may say that's already happening! But something seems to restrain us …

There's a wonderful quote that often gets ascribed to Albert Einstein that says, 'I'm just thinking God's thoughts after him'. In other words, we find ourselves in a universe of intelligibility, with laws that govern the physical realm. The very fact that we are able not only to discern, but also to explore and understand, these laws suggests that there is a design behind it all. And if there's design, is it beyond the realms of possibility that there should be a designer?

The Christian Union at my school was called 'The Paley Society'. It was named after a philosopher and minister called William Paley who once proposed this, saying something like, 'Imagine I was walking across a moor and my foot hit a stone. If someone was to ask me how that stone came to be there, I might answer that, for all I know, it might have been there forever. But now, suppose I found a wristwatch on the ground, I could not answer the same way, because the watch must have had a maker. It has mechanical moving parts and components. It must have had a designer.'

It's a simple but compelling piece of logic. And a key reason for why I personally feel that it takes more faith to believe that there isn't a creator, and that something just came from nothing, than that there is, and that that someone made something.

It strikes me that ultimately, only faith can allow for meaning. Only God can guarantee purpose.

I know it's hard to get our heads around the idea, but there's more to life than meets the eye. I don't believe you'd be reading this book if you didn't believe that. There's more to reality than can just be seen under a microscope. And there's more going on in the room you're in right now than you could ever have imagined. Because there's a spiritual realm as well. Unseen. Which is why it calls for faith. It's a realm that not only exists alongside the physical realm, but interacts with it and is indeed affected by it. By the choices we make, by the things we say and do.

And it's this realm that God dwells in. The invisible King of Kings. He speaks, it happens. He wills and it is done. It's as simple as that. Which means he willed for us to be! Isn't that amazing? For us and every part of creation. He made us to know him and enjoy his presence, to bask in and reflect his glory. Yes, we may have lost our way, but that's why he came to find us.

This is the bold claim I'm making (well, me and billions of other Christians and the Church throughout the ages!), that this is your true story. The one you've been searching for all this time. This is why you sense there's more. This is the key to unlocking wisdom and understanding, to finding spiritual answers and meaning.

I love how C. S. Lewis put it in the article 'Is Theology Poetry?' (published by Samizdat University Press): 'I believe in Christianity as I believe that the sun has risen: not only because I see it, but because by it I see everything else.'

In Jesus, light has come and he enables us to see. If you've felt in the dark, not quite knowing where you're going, why not give him a go, you might just find what you're looking for ...

Newness

We seem predisposed to love new things: new friends, new jobs, new clothes, new phones, newborn babies, new travel destinations – I could go on. There's something very special about new things, which is why every day is such a blessing. Pregnant as it is with new life and new possibilities ...

And then you stub your toe. Sorry, but you know what I mean. It's just all too hard to hold on to that grateful and optimistic attitude isn't it? Especially in Britain. Oh my goodness. We are just the kings and queens when it comes to cynicism. We love to tear things down and assume the worst. I generalise, but, on that theme, compare us to our American cousins. You Americans are naturally warm, and optimistic, and positive. At least Californians are! Maybe it's the weather ... in Cali and the UK too.

But (and I'm speaking to my British brethren here), don't you ever wish that you weren't as cynical or jaded? Don't you sometimes wish you were, well, more American? I mean, looking for the good, calling out the 'gold' in others, welcoming the success of friends as you would welcome it for yourself. I know I do. Now, I'm not the finished product by a long chalk, but I'm nowhere near as bad as I used to be. And the difference-maker for me? You guessed it – knowing there's a God who makes 'everything new' (Revelation 21:5).

I mean, how else can we deal with ageing, loss, disappointment or broken dreams? If you think this life is it, then when it's gone, it's gone for good. But when you have faith, when you know your creator can redeem, recreate and restore, that he can make all things new and has eternity to prove it, well, it takes a weight off the mind and helps you go with the flow. It's amazing to hear testimonies of how faith has helped people deal with the loss of finance, limbs or loved ones. I remember hearing Father Raniero Cantalamessa, Preacher to the Papal Household, teaching at our church holiday. He was citing the pain and suffering that we all go through in life, and how we often don't have answers, but he simply offered this: 'God's got all of eternity to make it up to you.'

As I've mentioned before and whether we like it or not, we all live out of a story. How we see the world and what we believe about it determines how we live. A life of faith enables you to hold on to hope and see the best in everyone and every circumstance. When you know how the maker of all things sees you – that he loves and forgives and accepts you – it allows you to love and accept others too. And when you know your future is secure, that you've got an eternal, resurrection body heading your way, it gives you peace about that grey hair, or wrinkle, or loss of shape, or bad diagnosis.

In the last book of the Bible (Revelation 21:3–5), John describes a vision of the future that he sees:

I heard a loud voice from the throne saying, 'Look! God's dwelling place is now among the people, and he will dwell with them. They will be his people, and God himself will be with them and be their God. He will wipe every tear from their eyes. There will be no more death or mourning or crying or pain, for the old order of things has passed away. He who was seated on the throne said, "I am making everything new!"

Doesn't your heart long for this? As we wrestle with and grieve over the state of our world, be it war, climate change, social injustice or economic inequality, don't we just wish things could be better? Well, here's the good news – one day, they will be, for all who believe and want in.

And it's because of this future that we can live with hope here in the present. Because no matter what comes, be it highs or lows, good times or bad, we can know where we're headed and that the best is yet to come. Not that we kick back and put our feet up – far from it. We work hard to partner with the one who is 'making everything new'. After all, he says he's 'making', not 'will make', so we get to join in with him here and now. Does he need our help? Of course he doesn't, but like a loving parent who lets their inquisitive toddler help shovel snow or wash the car, often more of a hindrance than a help (!), he loves to involve us in what he's doing. Be it matters of justice or healthcare, education or taking care of the planet, we're all invited to play our part.

Faith opens a new perspective: 'Therefore we do not lose heart. Though outwardly we are wasting away, yet inwardly we are being renewed day by day' (2 Corinthians 4:16).

When you know where you're heading and that it's to a kingdom of light and glory and eternal health and beauty, what can this world (or ageing!) do to you? Newness is coming, and it will never be taken away …

Oneness

There are moments in life when all feels right with the world. You get a sense of peace and oneness, like the stars and planets align. Often, it's on top of a mountain or on a beach as the sun sinks low. You're with people you love, doing things that you love, and it feels like life can't get any better. And then you stub your toe … again.

Why do I keep on saying that? Well, I suppose I just don't want us to drift into some sort of fairy tale or make-believe. Often that's what us Christians get accused of, but, you know, the amazing thing is that the Bible is as honest about the bad stuff as it is about the good. Yes, it speaks of an unimaginably glorious being who dwells in unapproachable light, who's all-powerful, all-knowing and all-loving – something hard to get our heads around – but it also speaks of the darkness and brokenness of humankind and what dwells in the human heart. It's realistic about the human condition and the world we live in. I think most of us are realistic too, but I'm stressing this just in case …

And yet there's something deep in the human heart that holds out for total connection and oneness. We inherently believe it must be possible. It almost feels tangible at times and yet simultaneously just out of reach. Do you know what I mean? We long to connect more with those we love, to communicate more, to know each other more, and yet, yes, you've guessed it, we always feel there's more. We look at a view, take in its beauty and colour, experience a sense of mystery and transcendence, but just wish that it could last, that we could somehow take it with us. Nothing quite seems to satisfy. Perhaps most importantly of all, we're aware of the niggling doubts and insecurities within ourselves. We often feel hurried, harried, fragmented and alone. And yet we dream of feeling one and whole.

Imagine a world where we shared a oneness with each other, looking to help one another as opposed to getting the better of each other. Imagine a world where we were more aligned and in tune with the natural world, alert to its signals and rhythms, taking care of our planet and all our fellow creatures. And what if we really could be united with our creator, learning to walk in step with him and hear his voice?

Well, in my experience, it all starts there. When you find reconciliation and oneness with God, you're able to find it with yourself, with others and with the world as a whole.

Because this is the claim of Christianity: that each of us was made for connection; for a relationship with our maker and the made; for a sense of unity and oneness nothing can disturb or undo.

What I believe we're truly longing for is what the Trinity enjoys. God lives in perfect, unbroken relationship – a unity of three persons: Father, Son and Holy Spirit in one being. Don't worry if you don't fully get it … it's a mystery that the Church has been wrestling with for 2,000 years! But, essentially, the idea is that they dwell in eternal relationship with one another. This is actually how we can describe God as love because they've always had each other to love, with the Father loving the Son and the Son loving the Father, and that bond of love being the Holy Spirit. It's pretty deep, hey? But it's amazing to think that love is behind and at the heart of our universe.

Through Christ, we are all invited into that eternal, life-giving relationship. Everything flows from faith. It's like being plugged into the mainframe or finding Wi-Fi when you had none. Life feels fuller, more meaningful, more connected, more joyful. Through his becoming one of us that first Christmas, being born in a stable in Bethlehem, God has eternally joined himself with humanity. The way of oneness with God has appeared. This means that when you say yes to his invitation to connect, you unite yourself with him forever. Walls come down. Guilt and shame disappear. Connection with life is yours! And your life will never be the same again.

You'll begin to see the world through a different lens; experience it with a different heart. You'll feel alive with the sense of what's possible and will always know there's more to come.

It's time to choose connection over disconnection. Oneness over separation. Just reach out and take his hand ...

Peace

~

Oh, how the world needs peace! Not just peace between people and nations, but peace within ourselves. And if the peace started there, where else might it spread? But where does peace come from and how can we find it?

I wasn't a peaceful child. Well, that is if you believe my mother (which I do). Apparently, I was 'hyperactive', a description often used to describe people diagnosed with attention deficit hyperactivity disorder (ADHD), though this condition wasn't well-known or understood when I was a child. I was always charging about, causing chaos. What was restless on the outside was increasingly mirrored and driven by a restlessness within, as the angst and quandaries of adolescence kicked in. Much of that is natural, of course, and part of growing up. But from about the age of 17, I just became aware of a general lack of peace within me. It's like I grew a conscience and began to feel the weight of my actions and words. And with that came a sense of guilt. Not false guilt, where we just end up 'feeling bad' but not really knowing why, but real guilt, about real things I'd done.

Until I came to faith in God, I didn't know where to go with that stuff, how or whom to say sorry to. I just knew I needed to.

But that's perhaps the greatest blessing of Jesus Christ – that he forgives us for the past. He takes the burden and sets us free. He comes and gives us the peace we long for deep down. Not just a moment's respite, but peace in our heart and soul.

One of the great privileges of being a minister is getting to preside over Holy Communion. It's the meal Jesus left us to remember him by, his offering up of his life for us all. Meals are times of fellowship and family, when people come together. After all, enemies don't sit down together, only friends do. And as we share that bread and wine, we remember his broken body and his blood poured out, to remove our guilt and bring us peace, to remove separation and bring us home. But, more than that, as we share that meal together, Jesus is truly present with us. He came to make us friends with God. He came to make us family.

When you know that peace, when you experience it within, it doesn't just transform you, it transforms your relationships, your world view and your ambitions. Nothing compares to it. Because the peace that God gives isn't just a moment's quiet or a settled inner world, good though those things are. No, the peace that's on offer is the very 'shalom' of God. Shalom is a Hebrew word meaning 'complete' or 'whole'. It's a word that can refer to a stone that's perfectly whole with no cracks in it, or it can refer to a wall that's made up of lots of bricks but has no gaps. It's a word that speaks of something that's complex, with lots of different parts, but which is harmoniously holding together. In other words, you and me! But not only us … our relationships, business dealings – all the different parts of our lives – too. Everything can be understood to dwell in shalom and be in alignment and balance, whole.

We live in a world where there is such division and strife,

where so much has broken down and shalom has very much been lost. The good news, however, is that all can be restored. That's what it means to bring shalom. Because true peace isn't just the absence of conflict, it's the presence of wholeness. It covers when nations not only stop fighting against each other, but start working towards and for the good of one another. Somewhat optimistic, you might think! And yet, this is what the prophets of the Old Testament looked towards, a 'Prince of Peace [shalom]' (Isaiah 9:6) who would one day come and bring reconciliation and healing to the world. Christians believe that this promised Prince has come in the person of Jesus Christ. He alone can bring us peace with God, peace within ourselves and peace with one another.

Before I came to faith, I think I lived as if the next success or goal would bring me satisfaction and peace and quieten the striving voice that was within me. So I'd push for that and, if I managed to achieve it, I'd soon realise it wasn't the answer – like a mirage in a desert that promises rest and refreshment, but is always just out of reach. Peace is something every advertiser in the world seems to hold out, or every coach or management guru, and yet it remains strangely unattainable. That's because peace isn't found in our achievements, it's only found in relationship with God. Or as the great fourth-century bishop Saint Augustine put it, 'You have made us for yourself, O Lord, and our hearts are restless until they rest in you.'

There's a wonderful scripture in Romans that says this: 'May the God of hope fill you with all joy and peace as you trust in him, so that you may overflow with hope by the power of the Holy Spirit' (Romans 15:13).

Are you looking for hope? Are you keen for more joy and peace? Do you want to know 'shalom'? Well, the writer here tells us that it's found through trusting in God. It's found through having relationship with him. And that kind of makes sense, right, because whatever we're connected to, the life of that thing or person, for good or ill, will flow towards and into us. So when we're connected to God, picture a kind of spiritual umbilical cord (bit weird I know, but I quite like this analogy!), then the life of God – here described as 'joy and peace' – flows into us, bringing us lasting hope. Connect yourself to the world's hopes of riches, beauty, power and fame, and they'll all end up disappointing. But connect yourself to God, and you're set for life, both now and in the age to come!

Perseverance

One of the challenges of living when we do is getting used to having everything on tap or at the touch of a button. Be it takeaways or holidays, box sets or instant communication, every area of life has been impacted by technological progress. Can you imagine what someone from just 100 years ago would make of life now, let alone 500 or 1,000 years ago? Incredible! And yet, I can't help thinking that, in all that progress, we've regressed in some ways too.

One of those areas is perseverance. I don't know about you, but I can be so impatient at times – I want things *now*, I want to be there *now*, I want to make progress *now* ... But, of course, I don't fancy the hard work that goes with it! I mean, surely there's an app for that, or a pill for this, or a 'life hack' for that? Surely there are ways of cutting corners?

However, while life has sped up in so many different ways, some things still don't come easy. Some things take work and dedication. And we are all going to need perseverance. It's not fun, it's not sexy, it sounds hard and it sounds boring, but my goodness how we need it in this life. I even feel the need to persevere in making this point!

Think about everything or everyone we celebrate in this

life, barring reality TV stars (sorry guys) – most of them have worked incredibly hard to get somewhere or achieve something. Be it our sports stars, or actors, or medical staff, or engineers, or artists, or scientists, or clergy (I'm kidding). When we stop to think about it, none of those people got there by just watching Netflix and ordering Domino's (that's a delicious takeaway pizza, for anyone outside the UK or US). I say 'just' because progress doesn't exclude those things, but my point is, hard work and perseverance are needed. Even Usain Bolt, the most talented sprinter in history, who famously ate 100 chicken nuggets a day while competing in the Beijing Olympics, had to do some training! And it got harder the older he got. So should we be surprised when you and I, who, let's face it, might not have quite the same level of natural talent as Usain, need to sweat more to get some results?

Life isn't easy – it brings challenges, opposition and battles. But if you've got a vision that you're committed to, if you know what you want to do, if you've got a dream you're going after, then all those things can be overcome. But it will take perseverance to make it happen!

Are you willing to work? Are you willing to fight? Are you willing to push through to achieve your goal? Neither am I … I'm joking! Yes, yes we are! Right? Stickability – that's what we need.

You know, the truth is, it's hard work being a Christian: fighting the fight, running the race, keeping the faith … it's tiring, and not without opposition. And sometimes I feel like quitting. Sometimes I'd rather put my feet up and just 'go with the flow' of the world. Ah, that sounds so good even as I say it! But then I stop to reflect on where I'm heading – to an eternity of joy and abundance, where the highest moment here on earth isn't even a footnote there in heaven. To a place where the streets are made of gold and a river of crystal-clear water flows, where the nations flourish and prosper and we are with God, face to face. That's where I'm heading, and that's where I want to end up, which means I keep my focus now and I get up when I fall. I try to discipline myself and I dig in when life gets tough.

My wife Kirsty is South African, which means things can get a little tense on big sporting occasions, especially when my father-in-law is around. I love her home nation. In fact, outside France, it's the country I've visited most in my lifetime, having been there five times. I went to mission school there on my gap year, and fell in love with the Cape and its people. Its most famous son, of course, is Nelson Mandela, or 'Madiba' as he was known. His inspiring story is truly one of perseverance in the face of evil and injustice. He committed his life to the toppling of apartheid, a system of institutionalised racist oppression that governed relations between South Africa's white minority and non-white majority for much of the latter half of the twentieth century. Part of his fight for this cause saw him imprisoned for 27 years. He spent the first 18 years of that in the brutal Robben Island prison, now a tourist destination. He was confined to a small cell with no plumbing and no bed and had to do forced labour in a quarry. Once a year he was allowed to see a visitor for just half an hour, and he could write and receive a letter just once every six months. Can you imagine? I mean, talk about pushing the human spirit to breaking point. And yet, despite all these challenges over such a long period of time, Mandela kept the faith and continued to lead the anti-apartheid movement from his cell. He even led a movement in the prison that saw the authorities hugely improve the living conditions there.

Mandela was eventually released and, following the dismantling of apartheid policy, swept to victory in the first ever multiracial parliamentary elections in that country. On 10 May 1994, Nelson Mandela was sworn in as the first Black President of South Africa. That is what perseverance looks like. He famously said, 'Do not judge me by my successes, judge me by how many times I fell down and got back up again.'

Now, you might not be leading a country into a new era of freedom and equality – neither am I. Your biggest battle today might look more like getting out of bed and just putting one foot in front of the other. All strength to you if that's so. Or perhaps it's persevering with a difficult child, or a marriage where the love's grown cold, or an ageing parent, or a thankless task or joyless job. Whatever it is, we all need perseverance. But it's only worth it because of hope. Hope that things will one day get better. Hope that breakthrough is on its way. Hope that the situation or person may change. Hope that 'this too shall pass'. So keep going, because you're not alone.

Prosperity

I like the word prosperity because I think it conjures up this idea of more than just money, more than just wealth – it feels more holistic. Now, it's important to say that there's nothing wrong with money per se. In fact, one of the most commonly misquoted scriptures is when people say, 'money is the root of all evil'. That's not what it says! The verse actually goes, 'For the love of money is a root of all kinds of evil' (1 Timothy 6:10).

A root, not *the* root! One among many. And not 'money' alone, but 'the *love* of money'. Gosh it's hard isn't it, because the truth is, we live in a world where money makes things happen. Money changes lives. Money makes the world go round. People live for it, die for it, kill for it, because it seems to control everything in life – it opens doors, it opens people, it opens futures – which is why it's no surprise that so many make it number one, putting it ahead of relationships, health and even God. People often put the cart before the horse and make money their first 'love', above all else. Which is why Jesus issued his famous warning: 'No one can serve two masters. Either you will hate the one and love the other, or you will be devoted to the one and despise the other. You cannot serve both God and money' (Matthew 6:24).

So, it's possible to get our relationship with money a bit skewed. Francis Bacon once said, 'Money is a great servant, but a bad master.' I think we all know that to be true. You just have to see the number of lives, relationships and homes that have been ruined by an unhealthy relationship with it. But it's important to be clear about something – God is not against making money. Some of the most prominent characters in the Bible have been some of the wealthiest to ever walk the earth: Abraham, Jacob and Solomon, for example. Almost everything Solomon drank from or ate off was made of gold, and we are told that silver was as common in Jerusalem as stones. Look out when you're next kicking one along the road ... What's more, prosperity was often seen as a blessing in the Old Testament. So there's nothing wrong with money in itself; it's our attitude to it that's the key.

And let's just keep in mind that God is the wealthiest, most prosperous being there is. Everything belongs to him anyway, it's just that he decides to give it away. He's the richest, but also the most generous. To think that God became a baby in an impoverished backwater of the Roman Empire! Are you joking? And all to demonstrate his love for us. There's a verse that says, 'For you know the grace of our Lord Jesus Christ, that though he was rich, yet for your sake he became poor, so that you through his poverty might become rich' (2 Corinthians 8:9).

Now, just to be clear, this isn't a guarantee of riches in this life, or material riches in general. This promise concerns the next life to be sure, but don't go thinking this faith game is a guaranteed pathway to health, wealth and prosperity – it's not. But what God does promise us is wealth and riches on the inside – a prosperity of the soul. The Apostle John went as far as to write, 'Beloved, I pray that you may prosper in all things and be in health, just as your soul prospers' (*NKJV*, 3 John 1:2).

You see, we all know from experience, and the testimony of the rich and famous, that money doesn't buy happiness. In fact, often quite the opposite. As Jim Carrey, the great comic actor, once said, 'I think everybody should get rich and famous and do everything they ever dreamt of so they can see that it's not the answer.' Instead, as people have testified down the ages, true wealth and prosperity happen on the inside, when our soul is at ease.

So, let me ask you, is your soul prospering right now? If not, could it be that you're looking for prosperity in the wrong place? And if so, would you consider coming to God, the lover of your soul? Because he alone can give you an inner peace that 'transcends all understanding' (Philippians 4:7). And when you've got that, well you'll be content whether you're a millionaire or barely have two coins to rub together. That's true happiness; that's true prosperity.

As the great German philosopher, Immanuel Kant, put it, 'We are not rich by what we possess, but by what we can do without.' We could all do with taking an inventory of that.

Questions

Every day we ask so many questions: 'What shall I wear?', 'What shall I have for dinner?', 'What should we watch?' (possibly the hardest question to answer ...) But then there are the bigger questions of life: 'Why am I here?', 'What happens when we die?', 'Is there any meaning or purpose to life?'

When I was 17, these were the questions that seemed to ambush me on an increasingly regular basis. And the problem with them is, once they start, they're very hard to stop. They're like a pebble in your shoe or an itch you've got to scratch ...

I can almost remember the exact moment when they started. I was standing in my classroom at school, and I just remember thinking, 'surely there's got to be more to life than just going to school and university, getting your grades, getting a job, making some money, spending that money, having a family (maybe), retiring, worrying about money, then dying?' I know there's more to it than that, but the question came into my head, 'What is life about?' And it was quickly followed by, 'Is there a God?'

It's funny, I was scared and thrilled at the prospect of God being real, all at the same time, because if he was, then it meant I could know him, and be changed, forgiven and find hope and purpose. I also imagined that it could only be a good thing to know the author of life and creator of the universe. But I was also slightly nervous, as such a being must be pretty awesome and powerful and so I wouldn't want to be in his 'bad books'.

So many questions ... but what I was delighted to discover was that there are so many answers too and that the Bible gives us many of them. I guess that's why it starts with, 'In the beginning ...' (Genesis 1), because God knows we'll all want to begin there.

Do you have questions? Maybe you're just beginning to have some new ones. Or maybe you're nervous to ask too many questions because you think you won't find the answers. Or you think the answers you do find might ask too much of you in response, or lead to conflict or division. After all, if one way proves right, what does that mean for all the other ways? While that's an admirably compassionate thought, it doesn't smack of quests for truth! Can you imagine Albert Einstein, when he discovered that $E = mc2$, keeping it quiet because he didn't want to upset Derek who'd always postulated that $E = mc3$? Science, or any other quest for truth for that matter, would have no truck with such an approach! Rather, let the truth come forth and the cards fall where they will.

But any inquiry starts with questions, and it's no different in the spiritual life. For me, those questions inevitably led me to ask, 'Who is Jesus?', the man who's behind the world's biggest religion and whom 2 billion people claim to follow. Once there, the next big question became 'Is he alive?' as the whole faith rests on the claim of the resurrection. Prove Jesus is dead and the house of cards comes tumbling down, but if he's alive, well, that has consequences for us all.

One thing I love about Christianity is how rooted in history it is. We can study this stuff and explore its claims – it's not just nice-sounding spiritual platitudes. We can ask questions about the history of it all, but we can also ask questions about how to deepen our prayer life and commune with this invisible God. It's incarnational, flesh and spirit. Which is helpful, because so are we. Which is why God put on flesh in Jesus Christ. He became one of us to come and better answer our questions.

My old boss Tim had a Labrador and would often say, if only he (Tim) could become a dog, they could communicate and understand one another better. Well, in a far more sublime sense, God did that in Jesus Christ. Unreal I know, but that's the claim.

Eighty-four per cent of the world has faith in some God or other. Which is why I find it so surprising when I speak to people who've seemingly no interest in spiritual things at all. More than that, it saddens me to think of people giving up on inquiry and questioning. Not about the physical world or visible creation, but about the invisible, spiritual realm. It baffles me that some seem to have convinced themselves that there's nothing there to be discovered. I'm always impressed when I meet someone who describes themselves as an atheist, because it just seems so bold. Agnostic I can understand, but atheist? I mean, have they searched the entire universe, looked behind every star and planet? Have they somehow managed to look beyond the universe, which is where, if I was its creator, I'd more likely be hanging out? I completely understand that people may be nervous, afraid even, to begin a search and discover nothing there, but how about we flip that round? What if you never searched, never questioned and missed out on what was always there? How sad would you be? How could you quantify missing out on the meaning of life?

Which is why it actually encourages me to see the spiritual

search of many, even if I don't personally agree with the path that they may choose. Because at least they're searching for something. And they're right to think there's more – more than meets the eye or can be seen or touched. Because we're not just flesh and blood, we're soul and spirit too. All the major faiths hold that out. As I always try to say when I preach: that spiritual hunger and thirst you feel … they exist because they can be met. Your thirst can be quenched, your hunger satisfied. You just need to know where to go.

Because good things come to those who question … 'Ask and it will be given to you; seek and you will find; knock and the door will be opened to you. For everyone who asks receives; the one who seeks finds; and to the one who knocks, the door will be opened' (Matthew 7:7–8).

Resilience

If there's anything that the last couple of years has taught us, it's the importance of resilience.

I remember when the Covid-19 pandemic started and it was a uniquely challenging time. We all experienced things together that we'd simply never gone through before. Things like lockdown, on a global scale. And as horrific as much of it was, there was a frisson of intrigue and excitement about being in the same boat, experiencing the same things. We saw people do wonderful things: here in the UK people like Captain Sir Tom Moore, a retired army veteran, who made headlines raising money for charity in the lead-up to his 100th birthday; NHS staff who worked relentless hours to treat the influx of Covid patients; people coming onto their doorsteps across the UK to 'Clap for Carers' every Thursday at 8pm during the early weeks of the first lockdown; and many, many more. And this wave of solidarity and neighbourliness seemed to carry us through the worst of it. Because I think we all thought this would only last a few months and then we'd be free. So when it went on for 6 months, then 12, then 18 … well, we started feeling pushed to the end of our tethers. Quite how parents survived lockdown with home-schooling, I'll never know! They should all be knighted as far as I'm concerned.

But it was extraordinary wasn't it, because it felt like we were all experiencing this shared consciousness moment with the common demands and challenges we were facing. And after the early months of this strange new world, there came a point when we were all just like, 'OK, enough now …' That's when resilience comes into its own.

And let's be honest, we all need resilience in life. I guess we could describe resilience as the ability to keep going when things get tough and to come back stronger when we get knocked down – like an elastic band's capacity to spring back into shape post-stretching, as opposed to being overstretched and going slack and loose. I don't know about you, but I've felt a bit slack and loose at times recently!

All of us are going to face challenges in life. It's simply the human condition. The question is, do we have the mental fortitude and internal resources to deal with them? I suppose, in this sense, you could call the resurrection of Jesus the most resilient moment in history. The world did its worst, condemning him like a criminal and nailing him to a cross, but he came back stronger than ever. What does that have to do with us, you might ask?

Well there's a prayer in the New Testament (Ephesians 1:18–20) that goes like this:

I pray that the eyes of your heart may be enlightened in order that you may know the hope to which he has called you, the riches of his glorious inheritance in his holy people, and his incomparably great power for us who believe. That power is the same as the mighty strength he exerted when he raised Christ from the dead and seated him at his right hand in the heavenly realms.

In other words, faith brings us supernatural power! This prayer gives us a vision of the cosmic Christ, high and lifted up, who has power and authority over all things. Jesus is King. He's the boss. And what this verse is saying is that the same power that raised Jesus back to life is available to all who believe. Are you looking for strength? Are you looking for help to persevere? Are you looking for resilience? Have faith. Look to God, who's overcome the grave … Think about it, if even death is no match for Jesus, do you think your relational troubles are, or the financial challenge you're facing, or your health worry, or anything else?

All I can say is that the hope that comes from knowing God is with me, and that nothing can separate us, brings me a freedom to face all my fears and the resilience to persevere, whatever life throws at me. When God's Spirit lives in your heart, there's a lot of available power.

Rest

We live in such a busy, hectic, connected world that, to actually get good downtime or rest, you need to be disciplined and deliberate. It's hard to switch off isn't it? Hard to find true peace or even its pal, quiet! I don't know about you, but sometimes I just get home and all I want to do is collapse on the sofa, switch on the TV and lose myself in something. But even though I love that, I rarely find that it gives me what I really need, which is rest for body, mind and soul. Is that even possible? And if so, how can we go about finding it?

Foundational to the Jewish people's way and rhythm of life is something called 'sabbath'. Christians practise it too. It's a day of rest each week devoted to the worship of God and spending time with family and community. And God sees it as so important that it's actually one of the ten commandments. In other words, it's basically illegal for Jewish people to work on it! Imagine that – one day in seven when you truly put your feet up, but also maybe your hands up too, in worship and prayer to your creator. Doesn't that sound good? Doesn't that sound healthy?

So many people struggle with stress these days, often brought on by overwork. We seem to have lost our bearings on a healthy work–life balance. And this can have a disastrous effect on our health, whether physical, through heart disease or obesity, emotional, with anxiety or depression, or relational, through angry outbursts or just not being there. A lack of rest and not taking time to prioritise the most important things in life can be hugely harmful not only to our own lives, but the well-being of those around us and wider society too.

One of the blessings of faith is coming to the realisation that we don't run the universe – that's God's job. So how about giving yourself a day off each week to appreciate and recognise that? And the funny thing is, you will undoubtedly be more productive and fruitful during the rest of the week, once you've had some rest. After all, if God rested on the seventh day, you can probably afford to as well.

So why not practise it right now ... take time to read these next words. And breathe. Just take a moment to stop. Quieten all your thoughts, your devices, your notifications and breathe.

We were created to know life in all its fullness, but sometimes we get those the wrong way round – fullness and life. That's where things begin to come unstuck, because a full diary doesn't always equate to a full life. There are rhythms we must abide by; seasons for everything under the sun. We must learn to live those rhythms again. So why not put in place a sabbath? It's not a law for you, but it's just good advice and it's a day that's truly blessed. It doesn't have to be a Sunday – it can be any day you like, but a day it should be and no less. You'd only be short-changing yourself otherwise.

Take time to be with family and loved ones. Take time to be still and relax. And remember, rest is not laziness. It's not doing nothing when you could be doing something useful. It's as much a discipline to help shape your mind as it is to restore your body. It's a day for reminding yourself, whether you have faith or not, that you are not in charge of the universe. It was here long before you arrived and it will be here long after you're gone. So take a day off from that job! You might even get better at your own.

But remember, as much as you might enjoy your work, you don't live to work, you work to live. It's hard to know life when lots of stress-related issues are bubbling up. So, take a step back. Pause. Breathe. And think about a new rhythm for your day, week and life.

Put first things first, and everything else will take care of itself. And when it all seems too much, relax, trust, rest. God's got this ...

Sacrifice

On 13 January 1982, Air Florida Flight 90 was taking off from Washington DC when it crashed into the Potomac River. It was winter and the river was full of ice. The crash happened near a bridge going over the river. The TV cameras could see everything. Millions of viewers, sitting in their living rooms, watched as a helicopter overhead let down a lifebelt on a line to a man struggling in the water. He grabbed the line, swam to another survivor just by him, clipped the woman in and she was hoisted up to safety. The helicopter let down the line again, and again the man did the same thing. He swam to someone else, and rescued them. He saved others before finally, due to the tail section of the plane shifting and sinking further into the water, he was dragged beneath the ice and drowned.

It's a deeply moving story. Made more so by the fact it's true. Something inside of us just loves stories about sacrifice; be it military epics, or family dramas, real life or pure fiction, it just doesn't get better than a sacrificial scene. Why? Because nothing embodies love more, and love is the greatest thing there is! Think of your favourite movies right now: *Lord of the Rings* with Gandalf ('fly you fools') falling into darkness, or *Gladiator* with Maximus taking on the corrupt Emperor

Commodus, or Dumbledore sacrificing himself for Harry Potter, or *Star Wars* with Obi-Wan Kenobi allowing himself to be struck down by Darth Vader, or *The Lion King* in which Mufasa saves Simba but gets trampled to death himself, or *Saving Private Ryan*, wow that one gets me, with Tom Hanks' character at the end saying to Matt Damon's character, 'Earn this'. Whatever film you think of, there's just nothing as beautiful as generous sacrifice on the big screen.

And hey, isn't this true to life too? In the small stuff as well as the big – I mean it doesn't always have to end in death! Be it a parent getting up for the umpteenth time for their crying baby, or a volunteer youth worker setting up that venue once again to reach the young people in their community, or an older sibling going without an ice cream because there are only two left and their younger siblings each want one, or the teacher, the nurse, the mechanic, the care worker, going the extra mile when nobody sees. We all know what sacrifice feels like, and we know it's the right thing to do. But why?

Well, at the heart of the Christian story is a picture of a God who gives. Who not only gives us everything we enjoy but in the end gives his life as well. Ask me why I'm a Christian and I'll tell you, 'because I believe it's true'. But ask me what I believe the most beautiful and love-filled moment was in history and, regardless of my faith, I'd say the cross of Jesus Christ. Because it's there that we see the clearest picture of sacrificial love. And it's no surprise really, as he'd taught his disciples, 'Greater love has no one than this: to lay down one's life for one's friends' (John 15:13).

You see, that's why I personally believe we love those stories so much. Because they hint at something bigger, an overarching narrative. It's like they're echoes of an original sound, revealing the shape of deepest reality. And that shape is self-giving love.

That's why it feels so good to give and truly put other people first. Regardless of faith or creed, that's just a universal truth. Which means it's written into the nature of things. And if you believe that, well you're not too far from faith at all! And that would make sense, right – that the creator would leave hints and clues about his nature in his creation and how life works. Yes, things are broken and messed up too, but that's precisely what he came to fix, so that through his sacrifice and broken body, he can put a broken world back together. It's what Christians remember at every Mass or Holy Communion – a divided world invited to unite around a table, sharing a meal together.

In his great allegory of the Christian story, *The Chronicles of Narnia: The Lion, the Witch and the Wardrobe*, C. S. Lewis captures something of the wondrous power of Christ's sacrifice and what it's won for us all. In it, Aslan, the huge lion who represents Christ, has offered himself and his life in place of Edmund, condemned as a traitor. Aslan freely presents himself to the White Witch in return for Edmund's release, whereupon he is bound, gagged, beaten and shaved. She doesn't just want him dead, she wants him humiliated, tortured and shamed. After this, he is dragged over to the stone table, where he is killed. The Witch and her forces then leave to prepare for battle against the inhabitants of Narnia. Unbeknownst to them, however, Susan and Lucy are hiding and tearfully witness the whole thing. They keep vigil that night, watching over Aslan's body. At dawn, when they turn to watch the sunrise, there is an almighty crack behind them. Upon looking back, they see the stone table broken into two pieces that run from end to end, 'and there was no Aslan'.

While wondering what it means among themselves, they ask, 'Is it more magic?' to which they hear a great voice from

behind them say, 'Yes!' For there, before them, is Aslan, even larger and more glorious than he had been before, with his mane intact once again. The children quiz him about what it means, to which Aslan replies that the Witch's knowledge only goes back so far, to the beginning of time, but that if she could just have looked back a bit further, before the dawn of time, 'She would have known that when a willing victim who had committed no treachery was killed in a traitor's stead, the Table would crack and Death itself would start working backwards.'

This is a picture of what God has done for us all in Christ. He's that willing victim for us – a perfect substitute in our place. He offers us hope, forgiveness and freedom. All we need to do is welcome him in faith.

Self-Acceptance

When I was a teenager, I had terrible acne. As far as I was concerned, this was a disaster! I lacked confidence enough as it was with the opposite sex, so adding that into the mix only compounded the issue. I didn't believe in God at that time, but if I had, I can assure you, I would have been shaking my fist at the heavens crying, 'Why Lord, why …?!'

Spots. I don't know why I've alighted on this issue to make a broader point, but I guess it's something we can all relate to. We grow up wanting to be accepted, desperate to fit in, longing for a blemish-free face, experience, career … whatever it may be. And then our first spot appears! And with it, existential angst. Everything has changed. The world seems a dangerous place.

Forgive the hyperbole, but there comes a point when we're all confronted by a shocking and stark reality … we are not perfect. The world says we should be. Magazines, movies, social media all espouse it, but in that horrifying first whitehead moment, we realise suddenly that we're not. And so we are then faced with a simple choice: accept ourselves, warts and all (hopefully not many of them), or begin a lifetime's journey and commitment to 'cover up', both of the concealing make-up variety and the concealing, protective 'walls around our heart' type. The latter are far more dangerous. Because if we go through life convinced that if people knew 'the real me', if they saw behind the curtain, if we let our pristine mask slip for just a moment, then we'd be cast adrift and rejected forever, then we will always be running, always be hiding, never fully known or at peace.

Perhaps that's where you are. Perhaps that's the life you're living right now. You're on a merry-go-round of make-up and 'made-up', be it stories, realities or identities. You've forgotten who you are. Or perhaps you've never really known. I know that place. I've walked those streets.

So how can we change the record in our heads and bring our true tune to the world around us? How can we find the confidence to be who we are? How can we live from, not for, acceptance?

Well, ultimately, as you might have guessed, I'm going to say it comes from God. Because, think about it, when we question and doubt ourselves, who are part of the created order, surely we can only find answers by going to the creator, if there is one …?

I believe there is. And if there is a God, then his opinion is the only one that really matters. For if he doesn't accept us, look out, because it doesn't matter if the whole world does. But if he does, wow … then everything changes, because his voice and opinion trump all others. If he made us, then, at the end of the day, only he can define us, because he knows us better than we know ourselves. And if he accepts us, then who cares who rejects us, because we're loved by the maker of all. As the scriptures say, 'If God is for us, who can be against us?' (Romans 8:31).

This is what I've come to discover and experience in my own life. Finding God wasn't just an intellectual adventure or exercise, it was a heart and emotional one too. Because something within us tells us there must be more, right? I mean, this world is just too beautiful, too magical, too sacred and mysterious to be here purely by chance. But more to the point, if we are here, you and me that is, then it must be because that same designer, creator, higher power, wants us here. And that's a life-changing truth to discover.

I often hear friends and family describe the God they don't believe in. Well, the good news, I tell them, is that I don't believe in that God either, because he's often portrayed as a rule-making busybody who's out to spoil our fun – a head teacher in the sky with an old-school cane, looking for someone to bust and punish. In some ways, I can understand how people get there. The Bible holds out a moral code for us to live by and God calls us to holy living. But what often gets forgotten in such descriptions and portrayals is the never-ending love of God. Jesus came to reveal what God is like, and his primary message is that he's a good and loving father – generous, kind and forgiving, who just longs to bring us home. You might feel a bit of a mess sometimes, God knows that I do too! You might not think that you're 'worthy' of God's love or good enough to come to him. That's certainly how I felt. But the amazing message that I heard, and the news that made it good, is that God's not put off by the stuff we think he might be. Quite the opposite in fact. Instead of turning away, he turns towards. Instead of rejecting us for our mess and sin, he's come to welcome us in his Son. That's the reason Jesus came.

There's a story told in the gospels of when Jesus visits the house of a religious leader. Halfway through dinner a woman comes in who's known to everyone there as a prostitute, a 'sinner' in the eyes of her society and thus someone to be shunned. And yet Jesus welcomes and accepts her, and because of the love and kindness she receives from him, she is moved to wet his feet with her tears and wash them with her hair. She then goes on to pour incredibly expensive perfume on them. (When was the last time you put perfume on your feet, or, better still, on someone else's …?) Why did she do that? Because of what Jesus had done for her. He'd welcomed her, not judged her, called her to a new life and offered her a fresh start. He'd shown her the heart of God and that, despite her past, she could find hope and a future. God still loved and accepted her.

Such an experience of grace and generosity has the power to transform us. It did with this woman, and it can with you too. True self-acceptance comes when we understand that God loves us as we are, even as he begins to change us from within.

So go easy on yourself. And know that if God accepts you with those spots and imperfections, who cares what anyone else thinks …?

Spirituality

Do you consider yourself a spiritual person?

For much of the last 20–30 years, many would have struggled to answer this question or, if pushed, would probably have said no. But that seems to be changing in recent years. There's been an exponential increase in the popularity of things like yoga, meditation, mindfulness and ayahuasca retreats. And even when people aren't engaging in those more direct pursuits, there has been a marked shift towards more openness to the idea of there being 'something' out there, or 'more'.

I don't come from a Christian or 'religious' home. None of my family subscribes to any major faith. And yet many of them would say they believe there's more. Some might even describe themselves as 'spiritual', especially my big brother, Will. In that sense, he's like many today who would say something like, 'I'm spiritual, but I'm not religious.' Kylie Minogue thinks that. At least she did when I asked her some 18 years ago. I met her in a bar and sought to tell her how much God loved her. I then asked if she believed in God and she said, 'I believe in spirituality, that we're all spiritual.' She speaks for many at this time. God bless you Kylie!

It feels to me like, where 10 years ago, many people described themselves as 'atheists', more and more seem to be taking the 'agnostic' route these days. Which means that they believe something's there, but they're just not sure what it is and so, understandably, won't put a name on it. But it's fascinating to witness, because, to a minister, it seems to indicate that there's something of an awakening going on.

Perhaps you feel it too? You sense there's more to life than meets the eye. That we're more than just physical beings; that we're spiritual ones as well. You feel it in moments of heightened sensory experience – a stunning view, a piece of music, a glorious connection with friends. Those moments just leave you feeling inspired and uplifted, like there's magic and mystery here; a spiritual realm interweaving our own. If so, I would humbly suggest that you're right. Indeed, we see that right at the beginning: 'Then the Lord God formed a man from the dust of the ground and breathed into his nostrils the breath of life, and the man became a living being' (Genesis 2:7).

Yes, we're from the earth. We're creatures, just like the rest of the animal kingdom. But there's something more to human beings. We have the breath of God within us. We're made in God's own image. We're spiritual beings, living souls, and we're made for so much more …

It's worth noting at this stage that the current condition or experiment of Western civilisation – that of seeking to do life and construct society with no reference to a god of any description – is unique in the history of mankind. Anthropology has discovered that in every tribe and people group that's existed, there has also existed the practice of blood sacrifice, be it animal or human, as a means of assuaging the wrath of a god or the gods. That alone points to the fact that humanity has always believed in a spiritual realm that somehow interweaves the physical one, for good or ill.

Every faith under the sun has an understanding of why this is and how this realm works. But, in essence, the Judaeo-Christian world view holds that it is this way because God is Spirit and he breathed his life into us right from the start. We were made for spirituality. The problem is that what the Bible calls 'sin' – the dark force that is at work within us making us do some of the stuff we do – desensitises us to God's Spirit, and instead enlivens us to the things of 'the flesh', our baser desires. The good news is, there's a means to be free and walk the way of God again.

There was a time when Jesus was travelling and stopped by a well to have a drink. His disciples had gone shopping or something, and he was there in the midday sun when a woman came to collect water. Now, the reason she came then, rather than in the cool of the day, was because she was an outcast from the community; a 'loose' woman whom we learn had had five husbands, something shameful in that day and culture. Jesus knows this; in fact he tells her it supernaturally, without her having told him. Yet, despite this knowledge, he engages her in deep conversation. It starts with him asking her for a drink of water, but it quickly moves on to him offering her 'living water': 'whoever drinks the water I give them will never thirst. Indeed, the water I give them will become in them a spring of water welling up to eternal life' (John 4:14). Not a bad deal, you might think! One of the reasons I love this story is it shows the compassion and grace of Jesus. He doesn't judge, although he could. He doesn't reject, although he could. Instead, he offers to meet her deepest desires and needs.

This woman had been looking to 'quench her thirst' in all the wrong places. Perhaps that's why she'd had five husbands already! And here was Jesus, saying he could satisfy her deepest thirst, and not just once, but on an ongoing basis. Later he said that 'Whoever believes in me, as scripture has said, rivers of living water will flow from within them' (John 7:38).

Doesn't that sound good to you? Part of what led me to faith was sensing that there must be more, that there was a spiritual realm 'out there'. But, more than that, I guess, deep down, I wanted a spiritual realm 'in here', in my heart. I believe that's what we're truly made for and where life to the full and lasting hope is found. This woman found it. I found it. And you can find it too, because it's found in Jesus Christ.

Success

We live in a world that idolises success – the rich, the powerful, the beautiful, the winners. From a young age, we are shaped to go after it, to position ourselves for it, to not give up till we get it. And in many ways this is a good thing: we want to do our best, we want to try our hardest and we all hope that, in so doing, we will meet with a measure of success. Yes, our parents may have told us, 'it's not the winning, it's the taking part that counts', but we all hope that's a mantra we don't have to apply to ourselves! Keep it in the back pocket, sure, but pray you don't need to get it out.

I went to the kind of schools where the marks of success were pretty clear and we were regularly reminded of them. From the age of seven, I was at a school where sports teams awarded 'colours' to the best players, prefects wore 'red guernseys' (to differentiate themselves from the masses, who wore navy ones) and the winning league (think Hogwarts with Hufflepuff, and so on) got to enjoy a feast with fun and games at the end of term. My senior school then had exclusive clubs with socks, and different trousers and coloured waistcoats for the prefects. Needless to say, it inculcated a deep desire in one's psyche to achieve those goals and lay hold of those prizes. I was no different; in fact, I was probably more driven, and woe betide anyone who got in my way. My identity became all too tied up with those trinkets and, even now, I experience pangs of regret or disappointment at missed targets or ambitions. I was also quite naughty, meaning that, even when I did get my hands on a 'red guernsey', I was demoted twice from the role!

Perhaps you can identify with some of that or perhaps it's a foreign world. Either way, when you stop to think about it, our institutions and society operate in similar ways, producing a competitive environment with the goal of generating best results – whether that's your boss at work pitting you against your colleagues for awards or promotions, or economic or polit-ical competition in society as a whole, simply trying to 'keep up with the Joneses or the constant social comparison generated by endlessly positive – and filtered – social media posts. The truth is, it's everywhere. And let's not beat around the bush; most of the time, it works. I'm not really disputing that. What I am questioning, however, is where it ultimately gets us and if it's really all we need.

Some of the most challenging words that Jesus said are these: 'What good is it for someone to gain the whole world, yet forfeit their soul?' (Mark 8:36).

Let's just play that out for a moment. We live in a world where people work almost every hour that God gives to take home a pay cheque that wouldn't secure them even a sliver of New York, Paris or Slough (the 'big three', I call them), and yet here is Jesus Christ, whom Christians believe is Lord of all, King of the universe, saying that, even if you were to gain the whole world, the *whole world*, as in every piece of real estate on earth, every raw material, stock and share, even if you were to gain *all* of that, and be the most successful person in history, it wouldn't be worth it if you lost your soul.

In other words, according to Jesus, success looks very different to what the world holds out to us. For him, success is primarily about stewarding, nourishing and holding on to your soul – the deepest part of each one of us. What's that worth to you, to me? Or what would you take in return for your soul? New York? Paris? Slough? Looking young for as long as possible? Being as rich as humanly possible? Finally 'making it' in Hollywood?

Let's be honest, we all know people who are seemingly 'losing their souls' for far less than that, working jobs that they hate for people they don't even like. I've heard of people who started hashtags saying #nodaysoff or #notimeforsleep. Terrible hashtags. It's a tragedy really. And it's theft ... although it's not, because people legally sell themselves, buying into this inhumane, soulless contract. But I say 'theft' in that I think the enemy of our souls has tricked us into thinking success, riches and fame are all that matter and that we should sacrifice everything else to get them. And so people duly do. Because when yoked to a 'godless' narrative, where we're all here by pure chance and there's no meaning or purpose to life, why would we prioritise anything else? 'Eat, drink and be merry, for tomorrow we die' is surely the wisest approach to take.

Not if we have a soul. And, if we do, success looks very different.

Now, please hear me (and Jesus and the whole Bible I think): this is not to say that doing well in life and having success is not a good thing, or that God is somehow against it. No, God is the most successful being there is! He wins at everything he does. He owns every resource in the universe (even Slough) and not even death could keep him down. God is a god of success.

But the beautiful truth is that he also accommodates the unsuccessful. He truly comes alongside the lonely and the poor and the broken – the 'losers' in this life if you will, which, when you have a true revelation of who God is and who you are, you realise includes you! He's a compassionate God, giving strength to the weak, which will one day include us all.

So, what does true success look like? It looks like prioritising your soul, putting God first in your life, others next and yourself last. It looks like the life of Jesus. And then, when the end has come, it looks like eternal life … miss out on that and not even the world will be enough.

Tomorrow

We spend so much of our time living in the future. Whether it's the big things like, 'Will I get married?', 'Where should I live?', 'What school should the kids go to?', or the smaller things like, 'What shall I have for lunch?', 'Where shall I go on holiday?' or 'What should I wear to that party at the weekend?' It's totally natural and I'm not saying it's wrong, but we can't deny that it uses up a lot of our time and energy and keeps us from living in the moment, being fully present in the present. And, when you think about it, that's really all we have. This moment ... right now ... there it goes ... and another one.

We've got to make plans, for sure. It would be irresponsible not to and life would be chaotic. I mean, without it, you'd just get to the airport for that holiday but would then realise you hadn't booked a ticket. We have to keep an eye on tomorrow and plan for it accordingly. Of course we do. But when it becomes a burden, when it begins to consume us, when it produces stress and anxiety because of its inherently uncertain nature, that is when we know we're paying it too much attention, when we're giving it too much of a place in our thinking, too much airtime in our minds.

Below is one of my favourite teachings of Jesus (Matthew

6:25–34). It's quite long, but the words say so much more than I ever could, so just take your time as you read them:

> Therefore I tell you, do not worry about your life, what you will eat or drink; or about your body, what you will wear. Is not life more than food, and the body more than clothes? Look at the birds of the air; they do not sow or reap or store away in barns, and yet your heavenly Father feeds them. Are you not much more valuable than they? Can any one of you by worrying add a single hour to your life?
>
> For the pagans run after all these things, and your heavenly Father knows that you need them. But seek first his kingdom and his righteousness, and all these things will be given to you as well. Therefore do not worry about tomorrow, for tomorrow will worry about itself. Each day has enough trouble of its own.

It's a fair point isn't it? I mean, have you ever seen an anxious robin or a stressed-out blackbird? To be fair, maybe they're inwardly terrified lots of the time, especially about their eggs, but they don't look it do they? I don't think they could sing as beautifully if they were. They just live a life of trust. This is the life Jesus encourages us to live – in the knowledge that we have a loving heavenly Father who knows what we need. Most of us have had parents who took care of our needs. Perhaps you're doing that right now with your own child. My wife is pregnant with our first as I write this! I know we'll do our best. Well, as good as human parenting is – it can't come close to the perfect fatherhood of God. And, as such, we can relax … we can say our prayers and leave the rest up to him. And that includes tomorrow. That's why I love what Jesus says with, 'Therefore do not worry about tomorrow, for tomorrow will worry about itself.' Take each day as it comes, he's saying, trusting that God will give you all that you need. Note that word, though: 'need'. It's not 'want'. Much of what we want is just that – it's more than we need. And if we think tomorrow owes us what we want, then that will lead to anxiety and disappointment.

So the invitation is to live in the present, one day at a time. Be mindful, pause for just a moment. Give it a go; you might find it strangely liberating.

Transformation

Do you ever long for change? I don't mean cosmetic-tweaks-around-the-edge type stuff, but fundamental life-shifting transformation. To become the person who, deep down, you truly long to be.

If I were to tell you that there's a way to become more loving, more joyful, more peaceful, more patient, kinder, better, more faithful, gentler and more self-controlled, would you be interested? I'm sure you would be; who wouldn't? We all long for those things in time.

Well, the wonderful news is that this is available to anyone who chooses the path of true spirituality, who welcomes Christ into their lives, because those qualities are the fruit of the Holy Spirit and will come about naturally in time.

Do you have plants or trees near you? Perhaps in the garden or in a nearby park? It's always exciting when spring comes around and we begin to see the flowers or fruit appearing. You don't need to force it or worry that it might not happen; every year the blossom comes, the flowers appear and the cycle of growth continues without fail. And it's the same in the spiritual life. When God's Spirit lives inside you, he begins to change and transform your life. He begins to shape us in his image and bring about the likeness of Christ in us. And it all happens naturally, or supernaturally I should say. The great Reformation figure Martin Luther basically said, while I sit and drink my beer, the word of God does its work. Sounds a pretty good deal to me!

Whatever your perspective on Jesus, whether you have faith in him or not, he is not a bad role model; indeed, many might say he's the best there is. *Time* magazine called him 'The most significant figure in history.' The Russian novelist Fyodor Dostoyevsky said of him, 'I believe that there is nothing lovelier, deeper, more sympathetic, more rational, more manly, and more perfect than the Saviour; I say to myself with jealous love that not only is there no one else like him, but that there could be no one.'

The Jesus we meet in the gospels is a man of courage, compassion, love and conviction, forgiveness, grace and joy. And the offer is there for us to look like him more, to have his characteristics in our lives.

When I came to faith, invited God into my life and experienced his love for myself, it changed everything. It wasn't that I signed up to follow a list of rules external to me, which were a burden and bore to fulfil. It's more like God's Spirit and presence came and filled my inner being, bringing a fountain of life from within. And once that spring of living water's been established, there's nothing you can do to turn it off. I went to bed one young man, fell asleep and woke up quite another! Everything had changed; I had been transformed from the inside out. A chap on the Christian holiday camp with me said the next day, 'What on earth has happened to you Pat, it's like you're a light bulb now!' And he was right. Where before the lights had been off and I was dull, now I felt fully alive and connected. Now that my roots were in the right soil, fruit naturally began to appear. Peace. Joy. Kindness. Patience (actually, I'm still waiting a bit on that one …).

And it's not just me. This has been true for millions of followers of Jesus down through the ages. Folks whose lives have been turned upside down – in a good way. And it's not just for us. That's the whole point of this book: I'm here to tell you it's there for you too, if you'd just reach out in faith and grab it. There's enough of God's love to go around. And just imagine a world filled with people who looked and lived increasingly like Jesus Christ …

I'm always amazed to learn about lives transformed. From the Apostle Paul, who went from persecuting the Church to being its greatest pioneer and advocate, to Saint Augustine, who left behind a life of decadence and promiscuity to become its greatest theologian. There's a story that tells of the recently converted Augustine walking along the street one time when he passed a lover from his past. She longingly called after him, 'Augustine, Augustine, it is I,' to which he replied, 'I know, but it is no longer I.'

The author of the hymn 'Amazing Grace', John Newton, which I played on my outings during the first Covid-19 lockdown, was a cruel slave trader in his earlier years. However, his life was dramatically transformed when the boat he was on, the *Greyhound*, hit a fierce storm while crossing the Atlantic. They thrashed about for over a week and none thought that they'd survive. In desperation, Newton, known as 'The Great Blasphemer', cried out to God to save him. The Lord heard his prayer and they were spared, with Newton going on to quit that dreadful trade and instead become ordained in the Church of England. His story was essentially captured in the first verse of his famous hymn. Why not give it a listen now?

But it's not just great figures from history whose lives have been transformed. I think of my friend Michael Emmett, who, in 1993, was busted trying to smuggle cannabis into the UK – the biggest haul the country had ever seen. Five tons of the stuff, worth around £13 million. He and his father, Brian, went down for 12.5 years each. Brian was a hardened criminal who counted the Great Train Robbers and the Kray twins as friends. But inside prison, their lives were changed forever as they both came to faith during a short service in the chapel. In it, they, and a number of others, were completely overwhelmed by the sense of God's presence in the room, to the extent that Brian was rolling around on his back, laughing. Mike says of that moment in the article 'Seeing the Light' in the *Sun* in 2021, 'What I felt was the presence of love, the presence of peace, the presence of hope. It just touched me. I stopped taking drugs straight away. Everyone thought I'd gone nuts.' Mike's gone on to sell flowers, a different type of weed you could say, and occasionally comes to my church.

Or Eddie, whom I've known for about a decade. Goodness, what a story. Eddie left school at 16 with no qualifications. He came to London and was sleeping rough on the streets. He became an alcoholic and then got addicted to heroin. He injected himself so much that he had no veins left and so had to inject himself in his groin, from which he got deep vein thrombosis. He had problems with his lungs, cirrhosis of his liver and very few teeth! He came extremely close to death. Then he went on Alpha (a course where people can explore questions about faith, spirituality and the meaning of life) and had a radical encounter with Jesus Christ. Someone prayed with him, asking the Holy Spirit to fill him, which he did. And Eddie was instantly set free from alcoholism and heroin addiction. He became a new man! A Christian dentist even gave him some new teeth. I remember being in the Royal Albert Hall for Alpha International's leadership conference and Eddie, along with other recovering addicts and people who'd experienced homelessness, was there too. For years, Eddie had slept outside the Royal Albert Hall under one of the vents, because it blew out warm air. But here he was now, sitting in the best seats in the house – none other than the royal box. Nothing could be more appropriate, because when the King of Kings becomes your father, you too become royalty. Eddie said, 'I can't change my past, but I can change my future.' And since that time, he hasn't stopped thanking God and serving in the local church.

Now, you don't have to be a slave trader, drug smuggler or homeless heroin addict, but all of us could do with some improvements! And transformation where you need it is possible. Fresh hope where you need it is possible. Because, with God, all things are possible. Just reach out and call on him.

Universe

'Thank you, universe.' I'll never forget my lovely mate who managed the café on the Portobello Road beneath our offices saying this. Not because I'd never heard those words before, but because I'd never heard them said together, with such faith and heartfelt sincerity. And, in that moment, I felt I had a glimpse into where much of today's culture is at in its thinking.

I could be wrong, but my sense is that 15–20 years ago, at the time of the 'new atheists' like Richard Dawkins and Christopher Hitchens, you could find a lot more 'out and out' atheists, those who don't believe there's a God of any kind. But, in my experience, most people nowadays would probably define themselves as agnostic – they believe there's something more, but they're just not sure who or what it is.

And I get it! I totally understand why people are hesitant, wary even, of putting a name on something or moving from the general to the specific. It raises questions of truth claims, exclusivity, unity and division, and more. So I totally hear my friend's heart when he keeps it vague, keeps it open, by saying 'thank you, universe' for a blessing that's happened in his life.

But, at the same time, I'm sure that most of us, him included, can understand the problem with that statement of faith.

Because the universe is part of creation; wonderful, majestic, unfathomable, yes, but as much a part of creation as you or me. And while it's a lovely attitude – to be thankful for all things and to bless all elements of creation – it feels like we come up somewhat short if we just do that but forget the creator. It would be a bit like some incredibly wealthy billionaire inviting you to take a holiday in their mansion on the beach. You enjoy the facilities, make the most of all it offers, but when you come to write a thank you note, you say, 'Dear Mansion, thanks for having me ...' How do you think the owner would feel?

Now the analogy breaks down, because God doesn't stand at a distance like this owner; instead he's come close and wants to be known. But, more importantly, it's less for his good and more for ours! We have been made for so much more – more than shopping, or scrolling, or bingeing TV series. We have been made for connection and relationship with the creator of the universe, for a life of worship that feeds and energises our souls. Yet we settle for so much less.

But why should we think there's more? Why can't we be here by chance? Well, yes, of course we might be, but let's just quickly explore the probability of that chance.

In 1966, the astronomer Carl Sagan proposed that there were two key criteria for a planet to support life: the right kind of star and a planet the right distance from that star. Seeing as there are around octillion (1 followed by 27 zeros) planets in the universe, it was reckoned that there should be septillion (1 followed by 24 zeros) planets that could potentially support life. And so the 'Search for Extraterrestrial Intelligence' (SETI) was launched, confident it wouldn't take long to discover E. T. and his glowing finger. However, as our knowledge of the universe has increased, so has our understanding that far more factors are required for life than Sagan first thought. Those two criteria went to 10, then 20, then 50, meaning the number of possible planets vastly decreased too, first to a few thousand planets, and then further still. In fact, the number hit zero before probability turned against the likelihood, going as far as to declare that even we shouldn't be here. And that kind of makes sense! Because there are now more than 200 known parameters required for a planet to support life, which must all be perfectly met. For example, a vast planet, like Jupiter, must be nearby to draw away asteroids, without which a thousand times as many would hit us. And yet not only do we exist, but we talk about existence – consciousness itself perhaps being the universe's greatest mystery!

Things get even crazier when we bring the fine-tuning data to the party. As Eric Metaxas wrote in the *Wall Street Journal*, 'Astrophysicists now know that the values of the four fundamental forces – gravity, the electromagnetic force, and the "strong" and "weak" nuclear forces – were determined less than one millionth of a second after the big bang. Alter any one value and the universe could not exist....'

Fred Hoyle, the astronomer who coined the term 'Big Bang', said that his atheism was 'greatly shaken' by this. He later wrote in the article 'The Universe: Past and Present Reflections' that 'a common-sense interpretation of the facts suggests that a super-intellect has monkeyed with the physics, as well as with chemistry and biology ... The numbers one calculates from the facts seem to me so overwhelming as to put this conclusion almost beyond question.'

It makes you think. 'Thank you, universe' is one thing. 'Thank you, Lord, creator of the universe' is quite another, and opens us up to a life of true spiritual connection. And that's possible because of yet more unbelievable stuff – because the creator himself chose to humble himself and literally become one of us.

Speaking about Jesus, John writes in his gospel: 'The Word became flesh and made his dwelling among us. We have seen his glory, the glory of the one and only Son, who came from the Father, full of grace and truth' (John 1:14).

In other words, the simple claim of Christianity is this: God, the creator of the universe, became one of us in Jesus Christ. We can know him. We can thank him. And one day we will see him.

Value

We prioritise what we value. Ask yourself: who or what is in your diary this week and why are they there? I guarantee you it's because, for one reason or another, you have assigned them value in your life. We do it to others, and others do it to us. And, for good or ill, this hierarchy of values impacts our sense of self-worth and even our mental health.

The world orders and structures itself as it does, creating clubs and cabals, with those who are 'in' and those who are 'out', all determined by the value placed on us. And, naturally, we end up wanting to be on the inside! It's human nature. For as long as I can remember, if I see a queue of people outside (or inside) a club, with a red velvet rope keeping them out, something within me wants to get in! I just hate feeling left out. I guess that's where the expression 'FOMO' comes from (FOMO stands for 'Fear Of Missing Out'). Perhaps you feel it too.

Now, of course, society needs to operate like this to a certain extent, just to avoid utter chaos and overcrowding, but where I think we get things wrong is writing people off on the basis of a flawed idea of 'value'. That millions of people go through life today wrestling with the experience of rejection, struggling for a sense of self-worth, because of what they've received or been told by the world, is heartbreaking. More than that, it's unacceptable and just plain wrong. It's a miracle every one of us is here! My agnostic friend would say, 'The universe really wanted you here.' I would say, 'God, the one who made you and loves you, really wanted you here.'

That's where my sense of value comes from – from knowing that God knows my name. More than that, he knows every thought in my head, every word on my tongue. He's delighted and interested in me. This is where true worth and value comes from. And this isn't just true for me – it's true for every single Christian, and it can also be true for you. Because that's one thing I love so much about the Church – it's a society of equals (or at least it should be). The ground is level at the foot of the cross. Every single person is invited and there's no red velvet rope keeping anybody out.

These concepts, or 'doctrines' as theologians would call them, have transformed not only how I see and value myself, but how I see and value others. The ultimate test for judging something's worth is how much someone is willing to pay for it. Well, here's the greatest truth of all: Jesus died for us. He shed his blood to buy us back. That's what 'redemption' means. It was the ransom price that was paid to set someone in bondage free. What are we worth to God? We're worth Jesus, his one and only Son.

Let that thought sink in – it has the power to change everything.

Vision

~

Do you have a vision for your life? A picture of where you want to go? A deep sense of what you're called to do and a commitment to focus just on that? One of the biggest challenges today isn't that we have too little choice, it's that we've got way too much! We've all experienced the 'analysis paralysis' that can come when we shop in a big supermarket. It's almost unbearable to be faced with a hundred different types of margarine! (We should all be eating butter anyway.)

It reminds me of an episode of *The Simpsons* when they turn up at 'Monstromart', whose strapline is, 'Where shopping is a baffling ordeal'. Some years ago, Tesco decided to reduce the number of products it stocks, just to counter this experience. There was a time when it offered 224 kinds of air freshener, while its competitor Aldi only stocked 12. Of course, on one level, it's wonderful to have choice, but on another, it can take us to a place of decision-making inertia, with us afraid of choosing the wrong thing. Afraid to commit to one brand. In such a milieu, where the world is our oyster, how on earth can we be expected to pick a lane and stay in it?

Well, this is where vision comes in. Because if you know where you're heading, what you're doing, what you're building, then you've got a compass for your bearings and you'll know what to say 'yes' or 'no' to. Whether it's building a house, a culture or a community, your vision and values set the course. They're the rudder for your ship!

Imagine if Martin Luther King, Jr. hadn't had the vision and convictions he carried. His speech might have begun, 'Well, I'm not quite sure where we're going and I'm not quite sure what we'll see, but it can't be worse than where we are now, so hey, let's just keep on keeping on ... ' Not quite as inspiring or galvanising as, 'I have a dream that my four little children will one day live in a nation where they will not be judged by the colour of their skin, but by the content of their character.'

It was Luther King, Jr.'s faith that inspired him; his understanding of God's heart in scripture that guided him and gave him his vision. And it was this that fuelled the civil rights movement in America. His speech ended, 'And when this happens ... all of God's children, Black men and white men, Jews and Gentiles, Protestants and Catholics, will be able to join hands and sing in the words of the old Negro spiritual, "Free at last! Free at last! Thank God Almighty, we are free at last!"'

We might not all be Martin Luther King, Jr.s, but the principle remains the same. As one of my favourite movie lines of all time goes: 'If you build it, they will come ...' (*Field of Dreams*).

People follow vision. Money follows vision. Action follows vision. As the Good Book says, 'Where there is no vision, the people perish' (*King James Version* (*KJV*), Proverbs 29:18). So let me ask you, how's your vision? Do you have one yet? No shame if you don't. And it's kind of hard to get one when you don't know what your purpose or the meaning of life is. But, as I've been saying throughout this book, that's a step you can take right now. Just start talking to your maker! Begin to follow him and ask him why he made you, what he's put you on earth to do. It'll be the beginning of a life-changing journey, where even the most banal task can be filled with glory.

Sir Christopher Wren came upon three men who were working on the site of St Paul's Cathedral in the heat of the day. He asked the first one, 'What are you doing?', to which the man replied, 'I'm laying some bricks and will be glad when it's done.' He asked the second man the same question, to which he replied, 'I'm making a wall to earn my keep.' But when he asked the same question to the third man, he was told, 'I'm building a great cathedral to the glory of God.' Life is about attitude and perspective. And everything we do is part of something so much greater if we'd just have the right perspective.

So, get a vision for your life and give it everything you've got! Whether that's setting up a new business or creating a home for your family, planting a garden or deciding to get fit, writing a book (!) or just deciding to read more of them. Aim at nothing and you're sure to hit it. Have a goal and vision and you'll make progress.

Vulnerability

It's been said, 'we might impress people with our strengths, but we connect with people through our weaknesses'.

Easy to say, but much harder to do! In a world that so often takes no prisoners, surely the wise way to live is through gritted teeth, with barriers up and defensive measures in place? After all, if Darwin is right and it is 'survival of the fittest', then showing weakness or vulnerability is the last thing I want to do.

Don't strength and gifts and power get rewarded in this life? To quote Jim Carrey's character from the film *The Mask*, don't 'nice guys finish last'? And, if so, why on earth would we want to finish there? Nope, I'm fairly sure that vulnerability is pretty much good for nothing, other than moments of intimacy with our other half when no one's watching and things feel disconnected. Then, it really works, but as a general rule for life, no way. Might as well put a bullseye on your back!

And yet … the studies and science seem to show that marriages and relationships are stronger, we relate better as people and organisations have more success when there's a culture of vulnerability within them – when partners let each other in, when friends truly reach out to and lean on one another, and when leaders are prepared to let down their guard.

But for this to work there needs to be a very high level of trust. Things need to feel safe and we need to know that what we share won't be exposed or used against us. Such spaces are hard to come by and, even when we find them, trust can be damaged or lost in a moment.

In its purest form and according to its highest ideals, the Church is supposed to be just such a community – where truth is held out and people are encouraged to bring all things into the light. One of its oldest practices is confession, where one person will come before another, often a minister or priest, and speak out into the light what's been hidden in the dark. The words or deeds they've done, or not done, that fall short of their highest ideals and the way God calls us each to live. The practice of confession can be one of the most healing and liberating moments in our lives, because it's only when you speak out that thing you're most ashamed of that you have the opportunity to hear that human agent speak back over you the very words of God, that declare, 'you are loved, you are forgiven, you are free'.

But it's only possible when you make yourself vulnerable. And it's ultimately only possible because Jesus made himself vulnerable on our behalf. Firstly, by taking on flesh and becoming one of us. That God would become a baby will never cease to blow my mind! But even more than that, that Jesus would choose to go to the cross for each one of us, carrying all the stuff that we've done wrong and often feel so bad about, is just too astounding for words. God the Son, being stripped and flogged, and crucified naked – talk about vulnerability. But that's the price of love! And it allows us to live a life of reciprocal vulnerability, knowing that we can do so safely, because we're held by 'the everlasting arms' (Deuteronomy 33:27).

My friend Tom is a recovering addict. He's been part of AA groups for years, which have helped him on his path. (To better understand the below, it's important to know that AA was founded on Christian principles and guests now refer to a 'higher power of my understanding' instead of God.) Tom had been sober for 10 whole years when he hit the buffers in the 2020 lockdown. Things got so bad that he took himself off on a six-week camp that specialises in getting people clean through the practice of the Twelve Step programme. One last chance, he thought. On the final day they shared their stories, and this is what he said:

I've prepared absolutely nothing to say. I was tempted to put 'lost property' at the top of the agenda as I seem to have lost quite a lot of stuff here, including about three and a half thousand tons of shame.

The week before I got here, I remember saying to my wife that I had no more good days to have or nice thoughts to think. I was about as depressed and broken as it is possible to be. I was at the end of my rope. I'd relapsed after many happy years of sobriety and the relapse took me from a gym-obsessed, healthy, well-adjusted man to the brink of madness and death. It did so in nine short months and it was, without a doubt, the most terrifying experience of my life. I don't know how I survived the last week, but I crash-landed here knowing that I had a mustard seed of faith and a window of opportunity, and I've grabbed them with both hands. And the transformation for me, over the last six weeks, has been nothing short of miraculous.

I have no doubt at all that there is a higher power, that he has my back, that he loves me, that he loves all of you, and I think that the higher power that I have faith in is enormously proud of each and every one of you. It has been such a privilege and a blessing to have shared these six weeks with you. I cannot put into words how grateful I am and how important you've all been and I'm going to miss you all so much. I want nothing but the best and finest things for you. You deserve it, we all deserve it. We are worth it. And if we work this programme we will have it. There it is.

Tom is a member of our church and his 'higher power' is Jesus Christ. When you have faith, a life of incredible courage and risk-taking opens up. But it starts with vulnerability.

Winning

If you're anything like me, you find it easier to look back and remember your failures than your successes. It's something of a curse and perhaps a mix of perfectionism and obsession, but it's also a consequence of society and conditioning. #winning – it's a thing! The world we live in loves a winner and, in the immortal words of Ricky Bobby from *Talladega Nights* (played by Will Ferrell), 'If you ain't first, you're last!'

It often feels like that, hey? But what a wretched way to live. What an unbearable yoke and demand. Yes, of course we must always do our best. We must make the most of the talents we've been given. And, when we do, who knows, we may win that race, we may get that job, we may ace that test. And we may receive the accolades that come with it. And there's nothing wrong with that. In fact, it's right and proper that we do, because winning at anything is part of life and should be honoured and recognised by all.

But the greater victory is having perspective and not letting obsession with it take hold. Do you struggle to let go of the past? Do you endlessly replay that missed opportunity, that failed attempt or that attempt not made?

I know I do. I still occasionally rehearse a football match

from when I was 13. We were playing our bitter rivals, another privileged private school, and it was 0–0. I collected the ball just inside their half and proceeded to go on a mazy run, beating four or five players, then sending the keeper the wrong way two metres out, creating the opening. But as I went to strike the ball, needing only to pass it into the net, the ball bobbled (I swear it did!) and I hit it with my shin, sending it just the wrong side of the post. I was gutted. The other team then went on to score the only goal and won 1–0!

Why does this still haunt me? Or perhaps I should ask, why do winning and losing, success and failure seem so ingrained in my psyche and soul? I don't know. But the more important question is, how can we be free to accept either one that comes?

There's an amazing poem called 'If–', by poet and novelist Rudyard Kipling. I encourage you to go and read it now – it's a manual for life. But it includes the following lines:

If you can dream – and not make dreams your master;
If you can think – and not make thoughts your aim;
If you can meet with Triumph and Disaster
And treat those two impostors just the same

The poem ends with:

If you can fill the unforgiving minute
With sixty seconds' worth of distance run,
Yours is the Earth and everything that's in it,
And – which is more – you'll be a Man, my son!

I love that line about triumph and disaster and treating 'those two impostors just the same'. Because the truth is, we're going to know both, and likely, plenty of each: highs and lows, breakthroughs and setbacks, success and failure. When you know that, it makes managing your expectations far easier and leads to a more balanced and less stressful life. And the sooner we realise we're called to run our own race, to stay in our lane and not worry about what our neighbour or that person over there is doing, because we're not in competition with them, the sooner we will flourish and become all we can be in what we're called to do. The polymath Albert Schweitzer said, 'Success is not the key to happiness. Happiness is the key to success. If you love what you are doing, you will be successful.' I love that! Be led by love.

And you know, I truly believe that the greatest victory in life comes when you know how much you're loved. Love is at the heart of this universe – God created us to know his love. And the wonderful news is, it's not based on our performance. We don't have to get straight As, or look perfect, or score that goal. Like any good parent, God still loves us when we come up short. He even loves us when we don't make a start!

And the good news is that, in God's economy, he can turn our mess into a message, he can turn a trial into a triumph and he can turn a victim into a victor. After all, it didn't look great for Jesus on the cross! And yet three days later …

What does winning truly look like? It looks like knowing that you're loved, both in this life and the next. When you've got that, then you've got a hope that cannot fail.

Wonder

Are there times when you just stop and realise the craziness of life? I mean, the fact that here we are, going about our lives – travelling to work, picking up the kids, choosing a filter for social media, comparing car insurance online – all the while doing it on a rock that's spinning round the sun, suspended in the vastness of what we call space.

I mean, doesn't that thought ever blow your mind? I come back to it again and again. Because, for me, it's the beginning of wonder. It's how I maintain a childlike heart and spirit. And I hope that, for me and my family, it will never be normal, never be boring, never be taken for granted.

I mean, what is going on? Why are we here? Where did we come from? How does it all work? One inch closer to the sun and the earth burns up; one inch further away and it freezes over. How does gravity work anyway? Or seasons, or light, or the internet …? Or babies! Sorry, but how ridiculous is it that mothers carry babies in their tummies? Growing them inside before it's time to come out. The whole thing is just too mysterious and wonderful for words. Right now, my wife is pregnant with our first child. Last I heard the baby was the size of a kiwi but already has their fingernails, brain, heart and lungs. I mean, ex-squeeze me? Is anyone else getting this?

Because the honest truth is that we should go round in a state of wonder and amazement all the time ... because everything's a miracle. It's just mind-blowing that things are here and they work! Albert Einstein once said, 'There are only two ways to live your life. One is as though nothing is a miracle. The other is as though everything is.'

And yet we so often lose our wonder. We get distracted by the things of life. Some very necessary, yes – like bills and bath time – but others less so, like endless online shopping or scrolling reels of strange animal behaviour. We get bored and take things for granted, ultimately forgetting where we are. Just to remind you, we are currently on a rock, spinning around the sun at approximately 460 metres per second or 1,000 miles per hour. No biggie then. And yes, I also have no idea why we all don't fly off into space, something to do with gravity apparently. But the point is, *wonder* should make us ask that! Wonder should keep us interested. Wonder is the only appropriate response to the absurd reality we call life.

For instance, did you know that a caterpillar has 228 separate and distinct muscles in its head? That there are 3,000 different species of tree within one square mile in the Amazon jungle? That the earth's core holds enough gold to cover the entire surface of the planet in 46 centimetres of shimmering metal (#bling)? That the earth travels through space at 67,000 mph, meaning you're 67,000 miles further away than you were an hour ago? (Ponder that one next time you don't think you've done much today.) That if you unravelled all of the DNA in your body, it would span 34 billion miles, reaching the planet Pluto and back six times. *Or* that almost all of ordinary matter (99.9999999 per cent of it) is empty space. If you took out all

of the space in our atoms, the entire human race would fit inside a sugar cube.

Crazy hey? It's honestly just mind-blowing. We are part of something beyond extraordinary.

So let me ask you, how's your wonder? And if you've lost it, can I suggest you reflect for just a moment on almost anything in all creation? The facts I just shared ... the tree you just walked by ... the flower outside your window .... the birds and the bees (that's not a euphemism, although there's majesty in both!) ... your hand.

Yes, your hand! Without opposable thumbs, we'd be nowhere. And keep this in mind – no one has ever had the same fingerprints as you. Wow. Totally unnecessary, and yet really rather wonderful. For me, it all points to a creator. I love what the great scientist Sir Isaac Newton said: 'In the absence of any other proof, the thumb alone would convince me of God's existence.'

I guess this all echoes what the psalmist meant when he wrote, 'The heavens declare the glory of God; the skies proclaim the work of his hands' (Psalm 19:1).

We are surrounded by such beauty and mystery. Let's just remember to keep our wonder.

X Marks The Spot

Can I get away with this one? I'll let you be the judge. But cut me a bit of slack – it was this or xylophone, and no one wants to hear that …

Do you ever go through life thinking that there's a plan A and, if you miss it, or mess up, or take a wrong turn, then you're on to plan B, or C (and then the rest of the alphabet)? Or, another way of putting it, do you sometimes feel you're searching for your truest life, your destiny, for the 'X' that marks the spot, which, when you find it, will give you everything you've been looking for?

I know I've done that before – become so convinced that one door is right, and my life and fulfilment are to be found on the other side of it, that if it doesn't open for me, there's no treasure for me and it's option B now all the way. This is an easy way to think, but it doesn't end well when we go down that path.

Thankfully, the story Jesus invites us into is a story of grace and forgiveness and fresh starts, where it's more like satnav than dead ends. One wrong turn isn't the end. Instead, with the all-seeing God on our side, he can just reroute us, saying, 'next left, second right, then you're there'. And over it all he says, 'Don't worry, I've got you.'

But the funny thing is, to begin that journey with him, to tune into his voice in the first place, we've got a bit of treasure hunting to do. Teaching about this very thing, Jesus tells a parable about the Kingdom of Heaven, telling of a man who finds treasure hidden in a field (he clearly found the 'X'); when that man found it 'he hid it again, and then in his joy went and sold all he had and bought that field' (Matthew 13:44).

Jesus is saying that he's the key to unlocking the meaning of life, purpose and the universe. That he's the way to the Kingdom of Heaven. And that he's worth giving up everything else in life to get. And that's certainly been my experience. Before I knew him, as much as I enjoyed life and all its many gifts and blessings, I sometimes felt like I was stumbling around in the dark, somehow missing the key piece to the puzzle. As strange as I know it sounds, finding Christ or, perhaps more accurately, allowing myself to be found by him, opened up a whole new world, and this time with the light on. It's like he's the door to a secret kingdom. Narrow yes, shoulder-width in fact, because it's through him that we go in. But when we do that, a grand wide vista opens before us and we enter the Promised Land. Psalm 18:19 says, 'He brought me out into a spacious place; he rescued me because he delighted in me.'

'X' really does mark the spot. Or, rather, not so much an X as a cross – the cross and resurrection of Jesus Christ, where all the treasures of the spiritual life are found.

During the Covid-19 pandemic, I wrote some words that we made into a poster and placed on the Portobello Road. I don't know why, but I feel it's right to share them here:

WHAT ARE YOU LOOKING FOR …?
A connection? An experience? A bargain?

A decent coffee ...?!

All of us are looking for something.
Whether success or adventure, great food or great fun,
relationship or meaning, freedom or forgiveness ...

But what if I told you that the secret to life isn't
found in our looking, but in letting ourselves be found?
What if I told you that the Creator of it all,
of the sun and moon and stars, of the rivers,
trees and sky ... was actually looking for us?

Because the amazing news is that, 2,000 years ago,
this Creator took on human flesh, became one of us,
to redeem that which was broken,
and to find that which was lost.

You might not be looking for Jesus Christ today,
but he is looking for you.
He loves you. He died for you! And he wants to bring you
home.

So if you'd truly find what you are looking for,
then let yourself be found.

Yearning

Do you ever just think, 'Is there more to life than this?'

I mean, more than the work deadlines, the endless news cycle, the traffic jams, the bills that need paying and the Netflix scrolling … Isn't the last one just the worst? It haunts me. Because I just know it's coming – every single time. And my wife knows it's coming too, at least when I've got the remote!

Growing up in a non-Christian home, I just didn't have a browser open for faith, and I wasn't searching for or googling it. For the first 17.5 years of my life, that is. But then something changed – I started having questions about the big things in life. Like, 'Why are we here?', 'Is there a God?', 'What happens when we die?' They niggled at me, disturbing my peace of mind. Alongside them, I became aware of a deeper longing, a yearning if you like, for truth, for meaning, for life … I became convinced there must be more. More to life than meets the eye. More to be experienced than I was currently experiencing. I grew aware of an inner hunger for connection, a spiritual thirst that just simply wasn't being met by the claims and offers of this world.

Speaking of this reality, C. S. Lewis says in the book *Mere Christianity*: 'If I find in myself desires which nothing in this world can satisfy, the only logical explanation is that I was made for another world.'

Just imagine for a moment that this was true – that there really was another world, another kingdom, which we were invited to enter and live from, even as we inhabit our own. This is the outrageous claim of Christianity – that our deepest desires and hopes and ambitions are able to be truly satisfied, not just in this life, but forever in the age to come. But it all hinges on one fact: the resurrection of Jesus Christ.

Professor Tom Wright, the former Bishop of Durham, says this:

> The Christian claim is this ... the resurrection of Jesus
> strongly suggests that the world has a creator, and that that
> creator is to be seen in terms of, through the lens of, Jesus.

All I can say is that when I took my first steps of faith, reaching out to this invisible God, inviting him into my life, he heard my cry and he came into my life. And that deep, deep yearning was met. That thirst was quenched, that hunger satisfied. Not that I've not known dry spells, or confusion, or times of unease and dissatisfaction since. But I've always known he's there.

As I've said before, I'm nothing special; I have no unique access that isn't available to everyone else. As the saying goes, I'm just 'one beggar telling another beggar where he found bread'.

And if you would find it, if you would admit that you're hungry and that the things of this world aren't filling you, then I just encourage you to come to him, the lover of your soul, the one our hearts desire. For only he can fill us up. Only he can satisfy.

Omega

So we've come to the end of our journey. A full stop if you will. We started at A and now we're at Z. The end of the road, or so it would seem. And, as we know, all good things must come to an end, right? We know this, we experience this: holidays, projects, relationships, life itself.

Well, here's where faith and Christianity really stakes its claim, because it issues an emphatic *no* to that statement. And it can do so because of the nature of God.

The final book of the Bible, Revelation, says: 'I am the Alpha and the Omega ... who is, and who was, and who is to come' (Revelation 1:8). 'Alpha' and 'Omega' were the first and last letters of the Greek alphabet.

Now if God is to come, if he is the 'Z', the 'Omega', then what looks like the end for us is just the beginning for him. The one who is and will always be, who knows the end from the beginning and has the power to raise the dead.

Do you feel like giving up? Do you feel you've had enough? Do you feel your race is almost run? Then come to the one who will 'neither slumber nor sleep' (Psalm 121:4). He can strengthen your hands for the battle. He can fit you for the task. Because he promises that 'those who hope in the Lord will renew their strength. They will soar on wings like eagles; they will run and not grow weary, they will walk and not be faint' (Isaiah 40:31).

The point is, with God, there is no end – there's no Z, no full stop. Just endless life and joy and glory. Isn't this the message of hope our world so desperately needs to hear? Scripture says that God made us 'a little lower than the angels' (Psalm 8:5). At our best and in our prime, we feel invincible. And yet life has a funny way of reminding us we're not and, as Chaucer wrote: 'time and tide wait for no man'. The years humble us. Old age ravages us. And we are left contemplating the end of the road, the last few letters of the alphabet.

Our house shares a wall with a Bupa care home, a place for the elderly, many of whom have dementia or Alzheimer's. There are times when we hear them crying out by day or night, asking for help or groaning in pain. It's heartbreaking to hear and a humbling reminder of the fragility of life. We may know strength just now, but one day that strength will fail, 'for dust you are, and to dust you will return' (Genesis 3:19). I've taken a number of funerals over the years. When the coffin is lowered into the ground, it all looks so final. And it is, unless Jesus also died, but came back again. Unless the Alpha and the Omega has looked our greatest enemy in the face and stared him down. Unless death is not the end.

And, as we close, what better place to land than with a word that says that, when all seems lost, it isn't; when all seems done and dusted, it's not; when it looks like a full stop, it's just a comma; when we read 'Z', God says, 'Let's go ...'

This is how ends can look like beginnings and a living hope can truly be ours.

Acknowledgements

Thank you firstly to everyone at Yellow Kite, Hodder & Stoughton and Hachette UK for making this book possible. Thank you to Lauren Whelan for taking a chance on this complete unknown! Thank you to Kate Craigie and Liv Nightingall for all your support, encouragement and patience (!) along the way, and Kim Nyamhondera for your work in spreading the word. Julia Kellaway, you were absolutely brilliant to work with as an editor. An older, wiser friend (who's written 19 books) said books are made in the rewriting, not the writing, and I can attest to that being true with your help! Thank you to Charlotte Trounce for your beautiful illustrations. They really bring those thoughts to life.

I also want to say a massive thank you to my friend and (now) agent Alice Saunders at The Soho Agency. I'd be lost in the literary landscape without you and would probably still only have written about 58 words if it wasn't for your gentle chivvying. Thank you for steering the ship and avoiding the rocks!

Thank you to Revd Canon Professor Richard Burridge for your theological counsel, ensuring there aren't too many heresies in the book!

Thank you to Mum and Dad for all your love and support down the years. You both enjoy books, so I hope you enjoy this one! Either way, you have to buy a copy I'm afraid. Thank you to Tones for always being there too. You might need the audio book by the time this comes out, or a magnifying glass! Shout out to all my siblings too – Anna, Clare, Jason, Millie and especially Will and Hubo, without whom I wouldn't be the man I am today. In many ways, this book is written for you, so please read it. (No skimming!)

The biggest thank you, however, goes to my wonderful wife Kirsty, without whom this book would still be nothing but a pipe dream. Thank you for your patience and generosity, allowing me seemingly endless days/evenings/weekends to write it. It's dedicated to our forthcoming baby girl, whom I only hope takes after you!

Finally, thank you Lord for this opportunity. You give me the air I breathe, the thoughts I have, the fingers to type with and the strength to keep going. You're the reason for my hope and I'd be lost without your love. So may this book say something about you and bring hope to all who read it.

About the Author

Photograph © Cait MacDonell

Pat Allerton grew up dreaming of becoming a fighter pilot, actor or surgeon. However, a spiritual awakening at the age of 18 turned his life upside-down and his journey towards the priesthood began.

Pat was ordained in 2010 and now ministers at St. Peter's Church in Notting Hill where he devotes his time to helping people explore life's big questions. Following the closure of places of worship as part of the nationwide lockdown in response to the coronavirus, Pat visited residential streets and hospitals in London on his 3-wheel cargo bike to deliver a hymn and a prayer through speakers. He became known as 'The Portable Priest' and is credited with spreading a message of hope in the city.

books to help you live a good life

Join the conversation and tell us how you live a #goodlife

🐦 @yellowkitebooks
📘 YellowKiteBooks
📌 Yellow Kite Books
📷 YellowKiteBooks